ADVANCE PRAISE FOR *HOARDING*

"Authors Gail Steketee and Christiana Bratiotis, internationally recognized experts on the topic of hoarding, deftly summarize the existing scientific and clinical information in this surprisingly easy-to-read volume. This book is a "must-read" for anyone who wants a better understanding of this complex condition."
—**David Tolin**, PhD, Director, Anxiety Disorders Center, The Institute of Living, Author, *Buried in Treasures: Help for Compulsive Acquiring, Saving, and Hoarding*

"*Hoarding: What Everyone Needs to Know* is an outstanding, easily accessible guide for anyone who seeks to better understand or assist someone with hoarding disorder. This book provides a thorough understanding of the disorder as well as practical guides for navigating housing, health, and other challenges faced by those with hoarding. The authors provide a road map for individuals with hoarding, their families, and communities seeking to better address this challenging issue."
—**Jesse Edsell-Vetter**, Director of Resident Services, HRI

"Steketee and Bratiotis have succeeded in producing a concise yet comprehensive overview of hoarding disorder. Summarizing over 25 years of research, this book is straightforward, easy to read, and an excellent answer to what you need to know about hoarding. It will be immensely valuable to those whose lives are touched by this problem."
—**Randy Frost**, PhD, Harold Edward and Elsa Siipola Israel Professor of Psychology, Smith College

HOARDING

WHAT EVERYONE NEEDS TO KNOW®

GAIL STEKETEE
CHRISTIANA BRATIOTIS

OXFORD
UNIVERSITY PRESS

Oxford University Press is a department of the University of Oxford. It furthers the University's objective of excellence in research, scholarship, and education by publishing worldwide. Oxford is a registered trade mark of Oxford University Press in the UK and certain other countries.

"What Everyone Needs to Know" is a registered trademark of Oxford University Press.

Published in the United States of America by Oxford University Press 198 Madison Avenue, New York, NY 10016, United States of America.

© Oxford University Press 2020

Library of Congress Cataloging-in-Publication Data
Names: Steketee, Gail, author. | Bratiotis, Christiana, author.
Title: Hoarding : what everyone needs to know® /
Gail Steketee, Christiana Bratiotis.
Description: New York : Oxford University Press, [2020] |
Series: What everyone needs to know® |
Includes bibliographical references and index.
Identifiers: LCCN 2019053078 (print) | LCCN 2019053079 (ebook) |
ISBN 9780190946395 (hardback) | ISBN 9780190946388 (paperback) |
ISBN 9780190946418 (epub)
Subjects: LCSH: Compulsive hoarding. | Obsessive-compulsive disorder.
Classification: LCC RC569.5.H63 S75 2020 (print) |
LCC RC569.5.H63 (ebook) | DDC 616.85/84—dc23
LC record available at https://lccn.loc.gov/2019053078
LC ebook record available at https://lccn.loc.gov/2019053079

1 3 5 7 9 8 6 4 2

Paperback printed by LSC Communications, United States of America
Hardbback printed by Bridgeport National Bindery, Inc., United States of America

CONTENTS

2 What are the common features of hoarding?   29

10 What are the next steps to understand and treat hoarding?   161

LIST OF TABLES

LIST OF FIGURES

ACKNOWLEDGMENTS

From both of us:
We thank our long-time OUP editor Sarah Harrington for proposing the idea of writing this book in order to educate various people with a vested interest in the sometimes complicated problem of hoarding. Of course, this work and our careers would not be possible without the great contributions of time and effort by many people who have direct experience with hoarding—those who suffer from its symptoms, family members and friends who are concerned about a loved one, social service professionals who are trying to help, and community professionals seeking to balance the needs of sufferers and the community at large. We are constantly impressed by the commitment of so many people trying their best to understand this problem so they can intervene effectively. More power to them all!

From Gail:
It has been a pleasure to work side by side (well, across the table) on this book with my delightful colleague and friend, Dr. Christiana Bratiotis. Writing it has allowed us to spend many hours and days together in her home in Vancouver and in my family's vacation home in New Hampshire—drafting chapters, talking about how to present the issues, and just catching up on each other's lives. Writing was interspersed

with walks in the woods, good food, visiting family and friends, and enjoying our surroundings. What an irreplaceable pleasure that has been.

I thank my delightful husband of many years, Brian McCorkle, who helped us by cooking great meals, being good company, playing piano for our listening pleasure, and supporting me in all my endeavors. I am very grateful to him for gifting me the time to work on this book.

I also thank my fabulous colleague, Dr. Randy Frost, for over 30 years of research and clinical collaborations on hoarding disorder. We have made countless trips back and forth between bucolic Smith College in western Massachusetts and traffic-snarled Boston and spent many hours presenting together at conferences and clinical trainings and in public forums. It has been my pleasure to play the role of "queen" to his outstanding "king" of hoarding—he is the best!

From Christiana:
I thank my treasured mentor and friend Dr. Gail Steketee for the invitation to collaborate on this project. During the hours of time Gail and I spent in collaborative conversation, writing, laughing, writing, idea generating, writing, editing, and writing, I regularly reflected on my good fortune to share the intimacy of this kind of work with someone so dear to me professionally and personally. The opportunity to be together in the same space to write (and play) with the scholar who "raised me up" in the field of hoarding was indeed a special treat of the most delicious kind. I will savor the goodness for years to come.

I wish to thank my family for their love and unending support of my professional pursuits. Most especially I thank my parents, Rev. George and Gloria Bratiotis, and my sister, Alexia Jobson, for reliably voicing their pride in my accomplishments and celebrating each milestone, large and small. I also thank my extended family—my brother-in-law, aunts and cousins, godchildren and their families, and my circle of friends who express sincere interest in my work and go out of their way to cheer me on.

Finally, I wish to thank Dr. Sheila Woody for being a once-in-a-lifetime collaborator and friend. We started our work together nearly a decade ago. Now, we have an ever-expanding program of research in hoarding, and I have the good fortune to work alongside a luminary who, by her example, inspires me to greater professionalism, optimism, scholarship, and good humor. Being just two buildings apart on the same campus, we have the luxury of seeing each other multiple times per week, including our standing lunch date! I thank her for her commitment to growing my career (and me) in the most patient, gentle, modest way imaginable. I am better for having her in my life.

Gail Steketee and Christiana Bratiotis

INTRODUCTION

In 2013, the American Psychiatric Association determined that hoarding disorder (HD) is a diagnosable mental health condition. This disorder has been studied only in the past three decades, although information about this surprisingly common problem has been accumulating at a great rate in recent years. In fact, published papers about hoarding have increased from 3 during the first half of the 1990s to 319 in first half of the current decade (2010–2015). This increased rate of published research on hoarding has continued in the past few years. In Dr. Randy Frost and Dr. Tamara Hartl's seminal 1996 paper on the "compulsive hoarding" syndrome, the authors proposed an explanation as to why people hoarded objects in their homes. Remarkably, the information they provided and their explanation stand up well today, even after scores of studies have been conducted on the psychopathology and treatment of hoarding. No doubt this information will continue to be updated in the coming years, but it provides a sound basis for understanding this complex and very serious condition.

HD is defined as excessive saving of objects and difficulty parting with them to a point that the clutter in the home interferes with the person's or family's ability to use the rooms and furnishings for their intended purpose. Excessive acquiring is very common, even when the home has little or no space to accommodate new possessions. Lack of skills to organize and store objects contributes to the disorganized clutter, sometimes to the point that only narrow paths traverse the cluttered rooms. This can be especially dangerous for older adults with mobility problems, and sometimes results in structural problems and fires that can be deadly for victims in hoarded homes. Even when not physically dangerous, hoarding behavior impairs functioning in many different ways, including inability to find important papers or items, excessive spending and debt, family conflict, legal and housing problems, and in severe cases homelessness.

Several studies across the United States and Europe suggest that clinically significant hoarding behavior occurs in 1% to 6% of the population, with a likely overall prevalence among adults of about 2.5%. This means that 1 in every 40 adults suffers from problematic hoarding, with an even higher frequency among older adults. This remarkably high prevalence rate raises the question of why HD is so common and whether Western consumerism and marketing might play a role in excessive accumulation of objects and difficulty parting with them. While there is limited information about why hoarding develops, it is a very serious problem that crosses cultures and socioeconomic groups and apparently spans the globe.

Why do people hoard, even when they suffer such serious consequences? One reason may be lack of insight into or awareness of their illness. Limited insight is common among those diagnosed with obsessive-compulsive spectrum disorders (OCSD), among which HD is included. Unfortunately, most people who are afflicted remain convinced of the importance and need for their objects, even when others around them disagree completely and there is compelling evidence that their acquiring, saving, and clutter are affecting their lives in a very negative way. Navigating sufferers' strong convictions about the importance of their possessions is especially challenging for mental health and other service professionals who are trying to encourage their clients to control the hoarding behavior.

The reasons that people who hoard acquire and save objects are actually the same reasons that most people do, but they are taken to an extreme in the case of hoarding. For example, common sentimental attachment to objects can become a strong emotional identification to broken or seemingly irrelevant items ("Getting rid of this [badly scratched] saucepan would mean I'm not a good cook"; "I can't really read this receipt, but it represents a day in my life"). In some cases, sentimental attachment involves anthropomorphism as the person ascribes emotional feelings to objects ("This stuffed bunny is dirty and torn, but it will be upset if I get rid of it"). Other reasons for saving include aesthetic attraction to the beauty of the objects ("I love everything purple. If it's purple, I have to save it"). Another motivation for acquiring and saving is the conviction that the object could be useful one day ("I collect broken furniture from the trash—someday I'll have the time to repair this and make it useful again").

Efforts to understand hoarding have led to useful theories that aid in developing treatments to address possible causes of hoarding symptoms. Among the ideas proposed is a "cognitive behavioral" theory that focuses on how people think and behave, and how these thoughts and behaviors influence their feelings. This kind of theory has been widely adopted and has led to hoarding-specific treatment programs. This treatment has been tested in individual and group formats, as well as in other delivery methods such as self-help books, peer support workshops, and computer/internet-based treatment in the home. This treatment includes strategies to enhance motivation and training in specific skills to aid thought processing that facilitates categorizing, sorting, and organizing jumbled piles of clutter. Other elements are practicing making decisions about whether to keep possessions in light of personal goals and taking action steps to remove unwanted items. This treatment has shown good success, but researchers agree that there is definitely room for improvement. Other theories for understanding hoarding behavior that derive from hoarding by animals and from the principles of economics might be helpful in expanding our understanding and treatment of hoarding symptoms.

In addition, as the impact of hoarding on communities is better understood, community-based interventions are also being developed and studied. Many communities have developed hoarding task forces that include providers of social services such as housing, public health, child and adult protection, animal protection, legal and court assistance, and other services. These service providers work together to develop guidelines and methods for referring individual cases and providing access to interventions and treatments that meet clients' needs. Research on these community and housing interventions is in the early stages and shows good promise for successful outcomes.

Many questions remain about what causes hoarding behavior and how to treat it. Hoarding runs in families and there is no doubt that genetic factors play a role, but what aspects of hoarding are inherited and how? We know that many people who hoard have experienced some traumatic life events, but to what extent are these traumatic experiences important in the development of HD? We suspect that interruptions in early emotional attachments to parental figures may be a factor in the development of hoarding, but little is known about how attachments to people affect attachment to objects. Cognitive processes are presumed to play important roles in the inability to sort and organize objects, as well as other aspects of acquiring and saving behavior, but researchers are still working to understand which aspects of the brain and its functioning are involved and how. How to maximize treatment benefits while controlling costs remains a special challenge for HD clients with limited insight and motivation and for communities with limited resources. These are only a few of the issues that challenge mental health professionals and others who are struggling to understand and treat this problem.

Hoarding: What Everyone Needs to Know aims to educate consumers, professionals, and the public about this complex problem, how it works, and what is known so far about how to treat it. Dr. Gail Steketee has conducted many studies on the nature and treatment of HD. She is a primary developer of the behavioral and cognitive therapy methods for this problem in conjunction with her close colleague Dr. Randy Frost. Dr. Christiana Bratiotis treats and studies hoarding disorder in the United States and Canada through the lens of social service providers and community task forces. She brings a broad professional, community, public, and family perspective to this book.

Chapter 1 describes the various symptoms of hoarding and the criteria for defining HD as a psychiatric diagnosis. HD's common features are described in Chapter 2, followed by a separate chapter on neurological (brain) features of this complex condition. Chapter 4 focuses on the adverse impact of the problem on sufferers and others. Chapter 5 describes ways to assess the severity and associated features of hoarding, while Chapter 6 attempts to explain why hoarding happens, at least to the extent that we understand it at this time. In Chapter 7 we examine various treatments for HD, including medications and especially cognitive and behavioral methods. Chapter 8 examines self-help and family efforts to reduce excessive saving and clutter. In Chapter 9 we turn to community-based efforts to resolve complex and severe hoarding problems that affect those living in the home, neighbors, and others. Finally, Chapter 10 raises questions that are not yet resolved in understanding and treating HD.

Additional information about hoarding can be found among the several resources listed in the back of this volume. These include books for professionals, for the public, and for those seeking self-help strategies, as well as professional journals that carry articles on hoarding and HD. We also list websites with useful information and a few web applications that may be helpful to people who suffer from hoarding. We hope this book enables the many people who encounter hoarding to understand the problem better and to feel empowered to provide help and recommendations for those in need.

1

WHAT IS HOARDING AND HOARDING DISORDER?

How is hoarding defined?

In a seminal article published in 1996, Drs. Randy Frost and Tamara Hartl described a syndrome they called "compulsive hoarding." They identified three main elements of this condition:

1. Excessive acquiring and failure to discard a large number of possessions, often items that appeared to be useless or of little value;
2. Cluttered living spaces that could not be used for ordinary daily activities; and
3. Significant distress or impairment in functioning because of the hoarding.

The primary feature of hoarding is difficulty letting go of possessions that most people would not choose to keep and that the person does not need, use, and sometimes even want. The kinds of items people who hoard save are not very different from what most of us have in our homes—clothing, shoes, magazines, newspapers, books, papers, pens and pencils, electronic items like CDs and videotapes, containers, kitchen utensils and cooking equipment, toys, and decorative items. In rare cases, a person may save unusual things like used tissues, their own urine or feces, and even old food and food wrappers. This type of saving can lead to unsanitary conditions in the home.

People with hoarding problems save objects for almost exactly the same reasons that most people do: for sentimental reasons, because they are useful, and because they seem beautiful. Chapter 2 provides more information about these reasons for saving.

Excessive acquisition

Excessive acquisition is a problem for the vast majority of people who hoard. Upwards of 80% to 90% of those who have lots of clutter actively acquire additional objects currently or have done so in the past. They accumulate by collecting free things and buying items, often at low prices at garage sales, used clothing and furniture shops, and discount stores. Some people roam their neighborhoods on trash collection day to pick up items they want. Once a person has a reputation for "collecting" things, friends and relatives may give them things they don't want, things the person with hoarding problems feels obliged to keep. Occasionally acquisition occurs through stealing, but this is rare.

Excessive saving

Excessive saving refers to the inability of people who hoard to part with their possessions. Once they acquire an item and it becomes an "owned" possession, they are reluctant to let it go. Discarding items into the trash seems especially hard for most people who hoard, harder than recycling them or giving them away, perhaps because of feelings of guilt about waste and concerns that the objects have meaning and value and shouldn't just be tossed into the trash. Unfortunately, such sentiments lead to saving items that most people would not keep in their homes.

Excessive clutter

Excessive clutter is the byproduct of acquiring and saving too many things that eventually fill up the household living areas and interfere with their normal use. Clutter is a defining feature of hoarding, but keep in mind that it is the *consequence* of excessive acquisition, saving, and disorganization rather than the cause of the problem. A hoarding problem significant enough to be diagnosed as a disorder requires the presence of at least a moderate level of clutter in the home. In moderate cases, furniture and floors are typically covered with piles of disorganized objects, but some parts of the room are still usable. That is, people can walk through the room and sit down, even if they have to pick up a pile to do so. In extreme cases, the person who hoards and other household members cannot cook in the kitchen, sit in the living room, or even use the bathroom because of the interference caused by too much stuff.

Disorganization

Most hoarded homes are disorganized to a point where similar items are not deliberately stored together and therefore can't be found easily. This means that important papers like car titles, insurance, and bills are mixed in among old magazines and other unrelated papers and objects. One woman, described in the book *Stuff*,[1] found an envelope with $100 in it when she shook out an old newspaper, because she had not separated the important and unimportant papers in her home. This difficulty organizing items seems to stem from problems with categorizing objects, paying attention, and making decisions, problems that are common among people who hoard.

1. Frost, R. O., & Steketee, G. (2010). *Stuff: Hoarding and the meaning of things*. New York: Houghton Mifflin Harcourt.

What are the criteria for diagnosing hoarding disorder?

In 2013 the American Psychiatric Association recognized hoarding as a unique disorder in the fifth edition of the *Diagnostic and Statistical Manual of Mental Disorders* (DSM-5). The DSM-5 categorizes hoarding as one of several obsessive-compulsive spectrum disorders and uses the same diagnostic code (300.3) that mental health clinicians use to diagnose obsessive-compulsive disorder (OCD). The DSM-5 identified the following criteria for diagnosing hoarding disorder (HD):

- Persistent difficulty discarding or parting with possessions, regardless of their value;
- Difficulty discarding due to a perceived need to save items and/or distress about discarding them;
- Accumulation of many possessions that clutter the active living areas of the home so rooms cannot be used as intended. In some cases, living areas have little clutter because other people intervene (for example, family members, authority figures);
- Hoarding symptoms cause significant distress or impairment in social, occupational, or other areas of functioning, including difficulty maintaining a safe environment;
- Hoarding symptoms are caused by other medical conditions (for example, brain injury) and are not better accounted for by other mental disorders like major depression, obsessive-compulsive disorder, or dementia.

In addition, clinicians are asked to specify *Excessive Acquisition* when difficulty discarding is accompanied by frequent acquiring. They are also asked to rate *Insight* as *good or fair* (the person recognizes that the hoarding is problematic), *poor* (the person is mostly convinced they don't have a problem), or *absent/delusional* (the person is completely convinced that their hoarding behavior is not problematic despite contrary evidence).

In addition to the American DSM system for diagnosing mental disorders, many countries use the International Classification of Diseases system developed by the World Health Organization. Version 11 (ICD-11) that includes criteria for HD that are very similar to the criteria in DSM-5, but excessive acquisition is considered a basic feature in ICD-11 rather than a specifier, and insight is rated in two rather than three categories (*fair to good* or *poor to absent*).

What distinguishes hoarding from other psychiatric and medical problems?

Accurately diagnosing HD as distinct from other psychiatric problems requires a careful assessment with special attention to the features of hoarding that are different from other problems. This process is complicated by the high co-occurrence of other primary mental health problems. Common accompanying conditions are discussed in Chapter 2. In addition to asking clients/patients about specific hoarding symptoms, clinicians might consult with experienced colleagues who can help determine the most accurate diagnosis. This is especially important for guiding decisions about empirically supported treatments for hoarding and other accompanying psychiatric problems.

Obsessive-compulsive disorder

Hoarding has a number of features that overlap with OCD. These include indecisiveness, perfectionism, checking, and doubting. It is not uncommon for people who are diagnosed with OCD to indicate during a clinical assessment that they also have hoarding symptoms. However, the reverse is not true—those with HD are less likely to also experience OCD symptoms like obsessions, checking, washing, and ordering. Furthermore, hoarding symptoms such as difficulty discarding and intentional saving are not strongly related to

OCD symptoms and tend not to respond well to the psycho-therapy and medication treatments that provide relief from OCD symptoms. This difference in treatment effectiveness re-inforces the notion that the psychological and biological under-pinnings of hoarding are different from OCD. In summary, it may be helpful to remember that although some people diag-nosed with OCD have hoarding symptoms and some people with hoarding report features of OCD, OCD is neither an indi-cator nor a symptom of hoarding.

Depression

In a study of people who met the criteria for a primary diagnosis of HD, Drs. Frost, Steketee, and Tolin found that over 50% of people with HD also met diagnostic criteria for major depressive disorder, which is characterized by low energy, poor self-care, changes in eating or sleeping patterns, and general disinterest in previously engaging aspects of life. When thinking about the relationship of hoarding and depression, the age-old "chicken or egg" question comes to mind. Although it is entirely possible that these two disorders are both present and are not related to each other, clinicians who listen carefully during a clinical inter-view can determine which one started first. If the symptoms of hoarding began before the symptoms of depression, the person is likely to meet criteria for a primary diagnosis of HD, and de-pression may be a secondary reaction to the debilitation caused by the hoarding (or other psychiatric) problems. If so, depres-sion is likely to recede after effective treatment of hoarding. The reverse is also true—if the person had symptoms of depression prior to hoarding symptoms, a diagnosis of major depression is appropriate, and it is less likely that depressive symptoms will resolve after effective treatment for hoarding.

Eating disorders

Hoarding of food sometimes occurs among people who have eating disorder symptoms such as anorexia and bulimia.

However, such behaviors would not qualify for a diagnosis of HD unless other types of items are also saved.

Psychosis

Schizophrenia is a psychotic disorder that is characterized by serious distortions in a person's perceptions, thoughts, and behaviors. These distortions include hallucinations and delusions ("positive symptoms") and social withdrawal (a "negative symptom"). Both types of schizophrenia symptoms can be associated with hoarding. Those with positive symptoms of schizophrenia often explain their hoarding behavior as motivated by delusional beliefs. For example, empty takeout food containers might be saved as protection from alien invaders. Excessive saving may also be motivated by negative schizophrenia symptoms when the person feels unmotivated to attend to the accumulating mass of possessions precipitated by their emotional disconnection to the world around them. In such cases, the person with schizophrenia may be unaffected by the removal of items from the home. Such motivations for saving are not consistent with HD as a primary diagnosis since emotional attachments are not the primary reasons for saving items and the loss of saved objects is not distressing. However, it is possible for a person to suffer from both schizophrenia and HD when both types of symptoms are present.

Dementia

Recent studies estimate that between 15% and 49% of people diagnosed with dementia have hoarding behaviors. That's a wide range that requires further understanding. Interestingly, people who hoard, both those with and without dementia, save similar types of items (clothing, paper, household objects), and when asked why they save the items, dementia sufferers with problematic hoarding provided the same rationale for retaining items as people who hoard but do not have dementia. Clinicians who listen carefully can discern whether cognitive decline is evident when defending their reasons for saving to others. Commonly, people diagnosed with dementia and hoarding will agree to let go of an item but later forget their decision, sometimes accusing others of stealing the very item they had agreed to discard. Tests of cognitive function, especially in older adults, can help distinguish hoarding as a primary diagnosis from hoarding secondary to dementia.

Brain injury

In a series of case studies of people who experienced brain damage, symptoms of hoarding appeared alongside other changes in personality and functioning following the brain injury. Specifically, the anterior ventromedial prefrontal cortex (brain region: frontal lobe, bottom of cerebral hemisphere) and cingulate cortex (brain region: middle portion of cerebral hemisphere) were the two most commonly affected regions. Collecting unusual items, difficulty making decisions, and poor judgment resulted. Recent research using magnetic resonance imaging (MRI) revealed that individuals with hoarding symptoms had damage to the mesial frontal region of the brain just behind the forehead. If excessive collecting and saving behaviors begin after an injury to these regions of the brain, a person is likely to have hoarding behaviors as a result of the brain damage rather than HD as a primary mental illness.

Is hoarding of animals part of hoarding disorder?

Dr. Gary Patronek formally defined animal hoarding as the accumulation of many animals without providing minimal standards of nutrition, sanitation, and veterinary care. In animal hoarding cases, scores to hundreds of animals are kept in overcrowded and unsanitary environments and are in poor health, showing evidence of disease, starvation, and sometimes death. It is not merely the number of animals that determines whether animal hoarding is present. Certainly, animal breeders and trainers may own or care for large numbers of animals that receive good care and live in healthy environments. In most cases, animal hoarding owners lack insight, denying that they have a problem caring for their animals despite clear evidence to the contrary. They show limited awareness of the harm they cause their animals, often declaring that an obviously sick animal was perfectly healthy or that the animal enclosure was safe even when the conditions were filthy. Many people who hoard animals see themselves as rescuers with special ability to understand animals.

The information in this section is limited because there is no standardized system to track animal hoarding cases and research that requires personal participation is difficult because those who hoard animals are accused of animal cruelty, a crime that makes them reluctant to volunteer. The frequency of animal hoarding in the population is not known, but information collected from a geographically diverse group of animal shelters suggests that 1 to 3 cases occur per 100,000 people annually. Animal control and humane societies report about 2,000 cases per year in the United States. Thus, this problem is far less common than the hoarding of objects. About three-quarters of people who hoard animals are women, a higher proportion than is commonly seen in object hoarding. Most are middle-aged and older and are not married (single, widowed, divorced).

When people who hoarded animals were compared to those who owned a similar number of animals that did not have health or environmental problems, both groups showed strong attachments to animals, urges to rescue animals, and similar histories of stressful and traumatic life events. A few differences were evident, however. Those who hoarded animals reported more chaotic childhood environments and difficult early relationships with caretakers, as well as more dysfunctional current relationships and mental health concerns. They were more likely to attribute human characteristics to animals. This suggests that people who hoard animals tend to experience more problems in their social life and carrying out everyday roles, and animals may be used to fulfill social and personal needs.

Efforts to understand animal hoarding behavior have indicated that it might be considered a type of addiction and/or a form of serious mental illness in which the person appears nearly delusional and unaware of their illness. Impairment in thinking and reasoning has also been suggested, but research is lacking to support these hypotheses about the origins of animal hoarding behavior. Of particular interest are theories that the dysfunctional attachment in childhood leads to intense emotional attachment to saving and caring for animals, accompanied by poor problem-solving efforts and difficulty coping. These intense relationships with animals strengthen the person's sense of well-being but also lead to intense concern about losing the animals for fear of personal disintegration and depression. Such theories have also been proposed to explain addictions, consistent with the idea that animal hoarding, and perhaps also object hoarding, may be a form of addiction.

The relationship between hoarding of animals and of objects is not entirely clear as there are overlapping features but also differences. From a frequency perspective, most people who hoard objects do not hoard animals, but those who hoard animals do tend to accumulate excessive clutter. Both groups show strong attachment to their animals and/or objects and great difficulty parting with them. Both have limited insight (awareness of illness), although this is especially problematic in animal hoarding. Both groups also have histories of stressful and/or traumatic life events, but this is also common to many mental health and substance abuse disorders. Those who hoard animals are more likely to live in unhygienic conditions, neglecting themselves and others living in the home and exhibiting poor nutrition, lack of medical care, poor personal care, and social isolation. This suggests that animal hoarding may share substantial features with domestic squalor, which is described below.

The Hoarding of Animals Research Consortium (HARC) is composed of researchers and practitioners from relevant disciplines in animal and object hoarding fields (veterinary science, psychology, psychiatry, social work, sociology, animal protection) who seek to understand why people hoard animals. At a meeting of experienced animal protection agency staff who had worked with multiple cases of animal hoarding, the group suggested that animal hoarding falls into three main types:

- The *overwhelmed caregiver* owns many animals that are reasonably well cared for until a change in life circumstances interferes with the person's ability to provide proper care. Events such as job or financial loss, death of a helping partner, failing health, and increasing social isolation may mean that initial efforts to provide care become overwhelmed, and living conditions deteriorate. The person is aware of and embarrassed by the situation and tries to minimize (rather than deny) the problem, but is often unable to comply with intervention by animal welfare authorities.
- The *rescuer* feels a strong mission to save animals from a perceived threat. They are afraid that their animals will die and are convinced only they can provide good care, even though the care is of poor quality. They actively acquire animals to rescue with help from a network of others (for example, animal rescue staff, community members who feed feral animals). Some rescuers falsely present themselves as staff members of shelters that care for animals. They typically deny health and safety problems and resist efforts by animal care authorities to control their animal population.
- *Exploiters* acquire animals to serve their own needs, with little true emotional attachment to the animals. They lack empathy for humans or animals and are indifferent to animal suffering, strongly denying any problems and rejecting concerns by authorities or outsiders. They exert

extreme control over their animals. The typical emotional attachment characteristic of overwhelmed caregivers and rescuers is not present. Rather, exploiters show sociopathic characteristics behind a charming presentation; they are manipulative, cunning, and narcissistic, lacking guilt or remorse. These are the most serious and difficult cases to resolve.

Unfortunately, research on animal hoarding is still too limited for experts to be confident of these categories, and of treatment strategies that have been proposed (but not yet tested beyond a few case studies). Much more work is needed to clarify next steps for this condition.

What's the difference between hoarding and collecting?

As noted earlier, some people with serious hoarding problems deny they have a problem and instead describe themselves as "collectors," attempting to legitimize accumulating more stuff. In fact, there are substantial differences between hoarding and collecting, as shown in Table 1.1. True "collectors" are able to clearly describe their reasons for obtaining new objects as part of socially shared activities that target special objects. This rarely leads to the distress or impairment experienced with hoarding.

Table 1.1 shows that true collecting is usually a shared and enjoyable social activity that does not impair a person's ability to function effectively at home or in their work and social life. In contrast, acquiring objects in the context of hoarding is often done alone and causes distress and debilitation across various life contexts.

Do people who hoard also have a compulsive buying problem?

Scientists have also studied a problem called compulsive buying disorder, which is characterized by frequent shopping

Table 1.1. Features of Collecting and Hoarding

Feature	Collecting	Hoarding
Objects	Cohesive themes; few objects	No cohesive theme; many types of objects
Acquisition	Planned searches; limited number of items; mainly purchased or traded items	Not planned; often excessive; free and purchased items
Organization	Items are arranged, stored, and/or displayed in an organized fashion	Items are disorganized and cluttered; often difficult to locate
Distress	Usually pleasurable; financial distress is rare	Considerable distress when parting with objects, acquiring excessively, and viewing clutter; financial distress is common
Social impairment	Low impairment; high marriage rate; collecting is usually a social activity shared with others	Mild to severe impairment; low marriage rate; relationship conflict and social withdrawal are common
Job interference	Rare; little work impairment	Common; may be underemployed or unemployed
Financial status	Cost of acquired objects fits within the person's financial means	May not be able to afford purchased items

episodes that lead to financial problems and interpersonal conflict. The individual is unable to control their urge to buy things, for example clothing and household items, to the point of extensive credit card debt and corresponding personal, work, and social impairment. Another problem, known as kleptomania, refers to stealing items from stores without paying for them. While kleptomania occurs occasionally in the context of HD (one study puts the incidence rate at about 10%), it is much less common than buying or acquiring free things. Both compulsive buying and kleptomania are considered impulse control disorders, a category of psychiatric disorders that also includes other impulsive behavior problems like chronic gambling, hair pulling (trichotillomania), and skin picking (excoriation disorder). For the most part, hoarding has not been strongly associated with these other impulsive behaviors apart from compulsive buying. Excessive acquisition of free things in hoarding obviously shares some features with these two acquiring problems, especially with compulsive buying, which often occurs as part of the overall acquisition problem in HD.

Compulsive buying appears to occur in about 60% of people who hoard, slightly more often among women (65%) than men (48%). When studied separately from HD, compulsive buying appears to occur mainly among young women in their 30s who are financially independent. Compulsive shoppers who see a desirable item experience a rush of excitement and often relief from negative feelings like loneliness or frustration. However, purchasing the item leads to guilt and remorse, as well as the pain of paying the unaffordable cost. Not surprisingly, excessive spending on unneeded items can result in closets and even whole rooms full of unopened boxes and clothing with price tags still affixed. Such behavior can become part of HD as acquisition is followed by difficulty parting with objects, leading to excessive clutter. Thus, a number of people with hoarding problems may also suffer from compulsive buying disorder that has contributed directly to their hoarding symptoms.

Does a messy or disorganized home mean there is a hoarding problem?

Hoarding behavior occurs on a continuum that ranges from mild to severe. A messy home with objects strewn about may simply reflect disorganized living and does not necessarily mean that a person has a hoarding problem or will develop one in the future. The inability to reliably organize objects is a hallmark feature of chronic disorganization, a chronic condition sometimes found among people who experience anxiety, depression, posttraumatic stress, and attentional difficulties as well as those who have had a traumatic brain injury. The Institute for Challenging Disorganization, a US-based group, offers support and resources for those struggling with disorganization and resources for professional helpers.

Many people who are chronically disorganized and others who have mildly cluttered homes for other reasons (for example, having multiple children) can and do invite family and friends over on a regular basis, usually after they've spent some time tidying up. By contrast, people who qualify for a diagnosis of HD may find it impossible to clear out the volume of clutter in a timely fashion and therefore rarely if ever invite people over.

Does a dirty home mean there is a hoarding problem?

Severe domestic squalor represents a problem of unclean living conditions that is separate but sometimes co-occurs with hoarding behavior. That is, regardless of the amount of actual clutter in the home, some people do not clean their homes regularly, leading in severe cases to filthy homes with accumulated trash, rotten food, unpleasant odors, and potential problems with mold, mildew, and insect or rodent infestations. This reflects a breakdown in standards of cleanliness compared to others from similar backgrounds who would find the level of cleanliness unacceptable. In severe cases, it puts the home dwellers at risk for health problems and the home itself at risk of neglect and being condemned as unfit for human habitation. Unlike HD, the accumulation of items is not deliberate saving but a result of neglect, a failure to remove trash and unwanted items, with no attention to the objects themselves. Because both hoarding behavior and squalor occur on a continuum, it can be challenging to determine whether the source of the dirty environment is hoarding or poor housekeeping, or both.

The early research on squalor identified it as a problem in older adults labeled "senile breakdown." A condition called Diogenes syndrome has also been described in relation to the elderly, referring to self-neglect in old age that has been associated with domestic squalor, physical illness, and sometimes dementia and/or severe mental illness. However, there is little consensus about whether these features constitute a syndrome, and it is not clear how or whether hoarding and squalor are linked to the other features. Hoarding of trash, called syllogomania, has also been identified in connection with these conditions. Domestic squalor has been studied fairly extensively. It affects both men and women and has been estimated to occur in approximately 1 in 1,000 older adults. Squalor can affect younger adults but is more common among those over age 65. More than half of people living in squalor have mental health problems that commonly include anxious and depressed mood, as well as personality traits of suspiciousness and social isolation. Psychosis with delusions and/or hallucinations and substance abuse may also be present. Some research suggests that frontal lobe abnormalities in the brain are associated with self-neglect and with a lack of concern for others that is commonly seen among those living in squalor. This is consistent with findings of impaired performance in executive functioning skills such as the ability to plan activities and retrieve conscious information from memory (working memory, verbal fluency) among people who live in squalor.

More research is needed to understand the development and persistence of domestic squalor, as well as the frequency and relationship of squalor to hoarding behavior. To date, researchers from the United Kingdom have suggested three categories:

1. Squalor because of deliberate accumulation of objects that make it very difficult or impossible to clean the home,

2. Squalor due to failure to remove dirt and trash, and
3. Squalor due to both problems.

Recent research suggests that about a third to half of people living in domestic squalor also exhibit hoarding behavior. The frequency of squalor among people who hoard is less clear but may be similar. Interestingly, relatively few people with HD who voluntarily seek help at mental health clinics are found to live in squalid conditions. However, among hoarding clients seen in community agencies, the frequency of filthy homes was higher, ranging from 40% to 75%, with the higher figure representing elderly clients whose physical limitations and cognitive decline may contribute to their failure to meet cleanliness standards. Animal hoarding studied in the context of public health offices is often associated with squalid living conditions, sometimes very severe for both the animals and people.

The research on hoarding and squalor identifies distinct differences between these conditions, although both may be present in a home. The random accumulation of trash and other items in squalid environments is quite different from the deliberate acquisition in HD because items are considered useful, sentimental, or attractive. People living in squalor also seem unconcerned when items are removed, whereas those with hoarding are quite distressed by the loss of objects. Squalor has been associated with dementia, brain injury, and personality problems, whereas object hoarding is more rarely linked to these features. The presence of hoarding plus domestic squalor will require significant intervention to resolve these personal and environmental problems.

Is saving electronic information part of hoarding disorder?

A number of people save a great deal of electronic information and files that they store on their computers or in other ways.

This has been called "digital hoarding" when the information is kept in a very disorganized fashion, and the person is very reluctant to remove any of the information and actively seeks out new electronic information. However, because such digital hoarding behavior does not clutter the living areas of the home, it is not considered a symptom of HD. So far there is much interest in this behavior in the media but little research is available to characterize the behavior and those who exhibit it.

Interestingly, some museum staff, especially those in history museums, have become concerned that their profession encourages excessive acquiring and saving of various electronic and historical materials as well as objects. While such behavior does not constitute hoarding as defined from a psychiatric diagnosis perspective, it does seem that the mandate of many museums predisposes them to accumulate more items than they can comfortably display or store within their existing spaces. Some museum staff have begun to try to resolve such dilemmas.

Why are some people unable to admit they have a hoarding problem?

As the diagnostic criteria for DSM-5 and ICD-11 indicate, unfortunately people with HD tend to deny that they have a hoarding problem, even when it is severe and starkly clear to family and friends. Or they may admit that they have a small problem and declare that they can clean up the clutter in a few hours, although that's obviously impossible. Many people, perhaps especially older adults with longstanding hoarding behavior, don't consider their behavior unreasonable, believing they are entitled to live however they choose, as they have for many years. Health department officials have estimated that fewer than half of the people whose clutter complaints they investigated admitted that they had a problem in their home. In one study, researchers found that more than half of family members believed their loved one had no insight about the hoarding behaviors. Some research suggests that people with HD have less insight about their problem than do people with OCD.

Denial of the problem is particularly troublesome for family members who want to help and for service providers who need to intervene. Even people who are threatened with eviction because of extensive clutter in their home may declare that they don't have a problem and should be left to live as they choose. It is also important to recognize that people who actively want and seek help for their hoarding problem inevitably feel ambivalent when faced with difficult decisions to part with their own possessions. Understanding why people who hoard lack insight or awareness of their problem is helpful as they consider whether to work on their problem.

In the context of hoarding and other mental health problems, "insight" refers to the person's degree of awareness that they have a problem or that it is a serious one. It has been called anosognosia, or lack of awareness of illness. This is a different use of the term "insight" than what might be called "cognitive insight," which refers to a person's ability to alter their previous beliefs in response to new information, as in "she helped him have new insight about how her mother felt."

In some cases, low insight might be due to mistaken beliefs. The person may truly believe that their possessions are valuable and important, no matter how much others try to persuade them it's not true. They may tell themselves they will eventually fix and use the broken chairs they picked up on the side of the road, although they have not done so in the past. They may believe that they should keep a badly torn stuffed animal because a child might want it someday. They may also believe that how they live is no one else's business, unaware that they or others living in or near the home are actually in some danger due to the clutter.

In many cases, people who hoard have become so used to their cluttered environment that they are quite surprised when photographs are taken and they can objectively see how much stuff is actually blocking the space. They have become accustomed (habituated) to the situation over time and no longer see the clutter as others do; they might be called "clutter blind." For them, insight may improve as they become more aware of how their home actually looks from the perspective of visitors.

In many cases, what appears to be low insight or insight that fluctuates with time is actually deliberate denial in the wake of strong pressure from authority figures or family members who threaten to clean out the home. It is not surprising that someone whose home has been cleared of clutter without their approval or participation would be extremely angry at the loss of control over their own possessions. Reparations and a very different and empathic approach are needed to help such individuals decide to work on the hoarding problem, which inevitably reappears after a clean-out in which the person who hoards has not actually altered their thinking or behavior.

Motivational techniques developed for people with addictions are especially helpful for people who deny that they have other mental problems, including HD. This requires a nonconfrontational approach while trying to see the problem from their perspective. Asking questions and making comments that express genuine concern and understanding of their perspective and experience can go a long way toward reducing denial and embarrassment about hoarding. Direct statements that show empathy help reduce defensiveness and encourage thoughtful consideration of changing behavior. Motivational strategies for hoarding are discussed further in Chapter 7.

What does hoarding look like in children?

Most of the research on children with hoarding problems comes from studies of OCD in children, so unfortunately there is limited information about children with hoarding symptoms who do not appear in OCD clinics. Children who hoard tend to collect seemingly useless items (for example, candy wrappers, old school papers) and report excessive concern about the location, care, and condition of the objects. They rarely accumulate the amount of clutter that adults do because their parents, teachers, and other caretakers control their acquiring, saving, and cluttering behaviors. Children commonly personify and personalize objects and worry about harming them. They may consider objects to be part of their personal identity so that discarding is an extremely distressing and traumatic experience. Some children try to prevent their parents or other caretakers from entering their room. Common features of hoarding in children are similar to those in adults— information-processing problems, emotional attachment to objects, and perhaps especially anthropomorphizing of objects, plus distress about the items and difficulty letting go. The information-processing problems, like those in adults, include difficulty with memory, planning, attention, problem solving, and task completion. Attention-deficit disorder may be present in children with hoarding.

Focus on: definition of hoarding and HD

Hoarding has been studied in detail only since 1990. It is defined as excessive acquisition and the failure to discard a large number of objects that appear to have limited value, so that clutter accumulates in the main living spaces of the home and causes distress and/or impairment in functioning. This definition has been incorporated into formal diagnostic criteria used by clinicians in the United States and abroad to define mental disorders according to two standard medical manuals: the DSM-5 and ICD-11. The diagnostic criteria in these manuals are very similar, differing only in whether acquiring behavior is a core feature of hoarding (as suggested by ICD-11 but not DSM-5). The DSM-5 also requires that hoarding not be due to other problems such as depression or OCD. Animal hoarding and object hoarding share some characteristics, but also differ in a number of ways that suggest animal hoarding is a more serious condition that stems from early attachment problems with caretakers and is accompanied by additional mental health problems.

Severe domestic squalor (dirty or filthy homes) also differs from hoarding behavior and should be separately diagnosed. When both are present, the condition of the home is likely to be more severe and treatment more difficult. People who deny that they have a hoarding problem may describe themselves as collectors; however, collecting has very different and more benign features than hoarding. Lack of insight or awareness of the presence or severity of hoarding is a common and particularly challenging feature that is likely to require treatment strategies that improve motivation to discard objects. Hoarding symptoms also appear in children, who often have intense concern about the object as if it were alive and about personal identity. Overall, HD can be readily diagnosed and is a separate problem from animal hoarding and domestic squalor, although it may be related to these conditions.

2

WHAT ARE THE COMMON FEATURES OF HOARDING?

How prevalent is hoarding?

Understanding the prevalence of hoarding is a complicated matter. To understand the research that has been conducted to identify the proportion of people affected by hoarding, there are several important distinctions to keep in mind. First, as a reminder from Chapter 1, there is a difference between hoarding behavior and hoarding disorder (HD). It may be helpful to think of hoarding as a set of behaviors that occur along a continuum from mild to severe, with the degree of impact depending on the level of severity. As described in Chapter 1, some people who have hoarding behavior meet criteria for a clinical diagnosis of HD. The diagnosis of HD requires a level of severity on the continuum that provokes significant distress or impairment that cannot be accounted for by other psychiatric conditions. Thus, those who meet criteria for HD constitute a subset of a larger group of people with hoarding behaviors. Accordingly, determining the prevalence of hoarding depends on whether participants are required to meet criteria for HD or merely have hoarding behaviors.

Another important factor that influences the calculations of prevalence is how researchers determine the presence of hoarding. Some population estimates of hoarding are based on reports made by people actually suffering with the problem, whereas others use formal standardized assessments by clinicians to diagnose hoarding. In addition, studies of prevalence differ in the specific method chosen to obtain reports of hoarding behavior. For example, some rely on visual inspection of the home to verify clutter, whereas others accept self-reported information about clutter. These differences obviously influence the threshold for what is considered hoarding and therefore generate variability in reported estimates of prevalence. Furthermore, studies may underestimate the prevalence when people are unwilling to participate because they feel embarrassed or stigmatized, as often occurs for those with hoarding problems.

With that understanding, studies have estimated that approximately 1% to 6% of people in developed parts of the world, mainly in North American and Europe, have hoarding behavior. In the United States, these estimates mean that approximately 1 in every 40 people, or 6 to 7 million Americans, have serious hoarding problems. Of course, the identification of hoarding is complicated by its multiple and complex symptoms and by variations in the threshold used to label the problem, as noted above. For example, mental health professionals are likely to use a conservative threshold that adheres closely to the definition in the fifth edition of the American Psychiatric Association's *Diagnostic and Statistical Manual of Mental Disorders* (DSM-5) and therefore requires a formal clinical assessment to determine whether the criteria for HD are met. In contrast, housing inspectors may use more liberal standards based on the degree to which hoarding generates health and safety risks. In any case, the estimates of the frequency of hoarding in the population make it clear that most adults know more than one person who has a significant hoarding problem.

Is this a new problem?

Two features of our current definition of hoarding—acquiring and intentionally saving items—have interested writers, physicians, and scholars since ancient times. In fact, the term "hoard" derives from the Old English word "hord," meaning "treasure, valuable stock, or store." Archaeologists have uncovered caches of objects dating back several thousand years in what is now Europe and the Americas, most likely hidden by hunter-gatherer groups to protect items they would need in future. This early human behavior mimics that of animals like squirrels and other mammals that survive due to their skills as "scatter hoarders" and "larder hoarders" (described further below). These caches, sometimes buried in containers, contained tools, weapons, religious objects, ornaments, and jewels, heralding societal notions of objects as reflections of personal wealth and status.

With the accumulation of wealth during Greek and Roman times, protecting that wealth became a critical need. In Greek mythology, dragons were given roles as protectors of golden objects and other valuable items. Greek and Roman literature and drama of this time portray character traits of miserliness that appear to reference hoarding behaviors. In the Norse saga *Beowulf*, believed to have been composed in the eighth century, a dragon seeks revenge when a human slave steals a gold cup from his lair of great treasures. Similar types of tales are readily evident in current-day writings and films. In the 14th century, Italian poet and writer Dante Alighieri refers to the problem of hoarding and squandering or wasting in his work *The Inferno*: "Then, in haste they rolled them back, one party shouting out: Why do you hoard? and the other: Why do you waste?"

Characters from Roman works made their appearance in Italian street theater. For example, in the Commedia dell'Arte Pantalone was portrayed as an elderly wealthy and greedy miser who stumbled about in a decrepit state like the depictions of Diogenes syndrome mentioned in Chapter 1. A number of miserly characters who sought to protect their treasure troves have appeared in many works since this time, among them Plyushkin in Nikolai Gogol's novel *Dead Souls*, a commentary on Russian society in the mid-19th century. Plyushkin collects seemingly random items on a daily basis, much like descriptions of current acquiring for people with hoarding problems. He collected "an old shoe sole, a woman's rag, an iron nail," which were added to the "pile in the corner of the room," and in his room he picked up whatever he saw—"a bit of sealing wax, a scrap of paper, a feather"—and placed them "on the bureau or the windowsill." Charles Dickens' Ebenezer Scrooge in *A Christmas Carol* has become a household word to describe a miser, and Dickens' character Krook in *Bleak House* collected and hoarded old legal papers, among dirty old bottles and hundreds of rusty keys. His liking for "rust and must and cobwebs" and refusal of "any sweeping or scouring" indicates that his hoarded space was far from clean.

In the late 1800s the psychiatric literature makes reference to patients with "collector's mania," now considered an early diagnostic label reflecting some aspects of HD. In the past century, perhaps the most infamous case of hoarding was the Collyer brothers of New York City. In 1947, Langley and Homer Collyer were found by police in their severely cluttered Harlem brownstone. All 12 rooms in their three-story home were filled floor to ceiling with an impressive array of things they had collected, including books, furniture, musical instruments, car parts, and simply junk. The newspapers of the time referred to it as "the palace of junk." It took weeks for city workers to clear the home, in the process finding both brothers dead amidst the hoard. The home was razed and the Collyer Brothers Park stands in its place.

While references to hoarding are readily available throughout history, the systematic scientific study of hoarding is quite recent. Only during the last 25 years or so have academics from fields of psychology, psychiatry, social work, sociology, and nursing begun to uncover the symptoms, origins, features, and manifestations of the problem. Even more recent is research into the neural and biological mechanisms that underlie hoarding and the development of helpful clinical and community intervention strategies. While our understanding of hoarding is growing exponentially, there are still many unanswered questions and much new territory to be explored.

Who is most at risk for HD?

A number of factors or vulnerabilities can increase the likelihood that someone will develop a hoarding problem. Among these risk factors are age, gender, education level, socioeconomic status, cultural and familial influences, genetic patterns, and life experiences. Below we examine each of these in turn, noting that no single factor will itself cause hoarding.

Age

Current research suggests the average age at which hoarding behavior begins is around 13 years. In fact, over 50% of people who hoard later in life report that their onset occurred between ages 11 and 20 years. When hoarding first appears in childhood or adolescence, the behavior is likely to be mild, and family members or teachers may intervene by requiring the child to clean up the mess, thereby limiting the appearance of clutter, at least initially. As more objects are acquired and saved over the next decades of adult life, the volume of possessions increases to a level that interferes with the person's ability to carry out ordinary daily activities. Researchers have observed the gradual worsening of acquiring, saving, and clutter to moderate levels by the mid-20s and to severe levels around age 35. Unfortunately, insight about the severity of the problem lags behind severity by several years. That is, those who have moderate symptoms in their 20s are unlikely to recognize their problem for another 10 or more years, and those with severe symptoms in their 30s don't grasp the gravity of their situation until their 40s. These findings may change with the greater publicity hoarding has received in the media and as awareness of strategies to address the problem increases.

Hoarding is a chronic condition that usually worsens across the person's lifetime unless effective treatments are implemented. Older adults with hoarding report a steady worsening of symptoms as they age, especially with regard to the accumulation of clutter. This may simply be a continuation of increasing symptoms over the lifetime and/or may also reflect declining physical and cognitive capacity to manage items in their home. Consistent with the delayed recognition of the problem, it is quite common for someone with even severe hoarding to wait until age 50 or later to seek help for their problem. Help-seeking typically occurs when the difficulty of using the rooms in their home for the intended purpose and carrying out everyday life activities (for example, being able to shower or cook) reaches a flashpoint. The intervention of loved ones is also often a significant factor in convincing someone to seek help. It is worth noting that many people never seek help for their hoarding, a topic we discuss at greater length in Chapter 10.

Gender

Some estimates indicate that the prevalence of hoarding is slightly higher among men than women in binary gender reporting. The samples studied to obtain these estimates are likely to influence the findings. Higher rates of men than women with hoarding were found in prevalence studies based on large populations, whereas other reports of the occurrence of hoarding show similar rates for men and women. For example, one study estimated the prevalence for men at 49% and for women at 51%. Women with hoarding appear to be more willing to seek treatment and tend to be represented more often among participants in mental health research compared to community and population studies. Indeed, women seek treatment more often than men do for a number of mental and physical health conditions.

Education and economic status

Hoarding behavior occurs among people from a wide range of educational and economic backgrounds. There is no apparent direct relationship between developing a hoarding problem and these factors. However, people with serious hoarding problems often experience economic hardship as a result of their hoarding behavior. Financial difficulty can result from overspending during excessive acquiring, from hoarding behavior at work (for example, excessive acquiring, disorganized clutter) that leads to job loss, and from missed days at work due to other consequences of hoarding. At the same time, people with greater education and wealth are more likely to have access to resources that help them resolve their hoarding behavior. Recent research suggests that economic status is associated with the presence of squalor—those with limited financial resources who hoard are more likely to live in conditions of squalor.

Family and culture

From a demographic perspective, a surprisingly large portion of people with hoarding problems live alone and have never married or are currently divorced, compared to the population as a whole. In a large internet study, researchers found that a little over half of those with self-reported hoarding problems were married or living with someone and about 45% were single, divorced, or widowed. Among older adults, somewhere between one-third and one-half reported that they had never married, and only about 20% were currently married, perhaps because being widowed is more common in such groups. Several studies confirm that people who hoard are less likely to be married and more likely to live alone compared to people with other psychiatric disorders and to community members without such problems. On rare occasions, hoarding behavior may be evident in both members of a couple or in sibling pairs where both are actively participating in excessive acquiring and saving activities. Such dual hoarding problems can be especially challenging to resolve as each person is socially supported in their problematic symptoms.

Some people who hoard choose to live a socially isolated life with limited contact with family members and few friends, whereas others are quite social, maintaining friendships and social activities that bring them into regular contact with other people. Certainly many people with hoarding problems are too embarrassed to invite people into their cluttered homes, and some have lost marriages and relationships because the spouse/partner could not tolerate living in a hoarded home. It is not clear whether hoarding behavior for some people is a way to avoid social contact or whether their social isolation is caused by excessive attachment to objects that prevents them from keeping a tidy home.

Family norms and behavior patterns do appear to influence the development of hoarding symptoms beyond genetic factors (see below). That is, the beliefs and values that guide behavior are transmitted to family members both overtly (for example, through discussion) and covertly (through observed actions and family reactions to behaviors). Hoarding behaviors are likely to be influenced by expectations about cleanliness, orderliness, and waste, and accordingly, answers to questions such as, "How much is too much?" will vary.

There has been limited scientific exploration of the influences of ethnicity or national origin on the development of hoarding. The countries where hoarding has been studied most widely are in the global north (European and North American countries), where hoarding appears to be fairly widespread. To date, reports about hoarding have also appeared in other parts of the world, including Asia (China, Japan, Korea), South America (Brazil), South Asia (India), and the Middle East (Turkey, Iran). The very limited research on cultural differences in hoarding symptoms generally suggests that the symptoms, characteristics, and frequency of hoarding are similar across cultures.

At the same time, we have little information about whether there are observable cultural variations in what types of items are saved and how they accumulate in the home environment. Likewise, we know little about whether cultural background is a risk factor for hoarding problems. There may be some differences across cultures regarding the reasons for saving items. For example, in China, usefulness and wastefulness were primary reasons for saving, compared to the sentimental interests that were evident for people who hoarded in the United Kingdom and in Brazil.

Genetics and family history

The effort to understand the genetic underpinnings of hoarding is a rapidly expanding area of scientific study. Advances in genetic technologies and approaches to finding and testing genes, combined with an increased interest in the genetic understanding of psychiatric disorders, has led to some useful findings related to hoarding. Heritability studies have identified six chromosomal markers for a hoarding-related trait, although this work is still in its infancy. Researchers suggest that genetic factors can account for approximately half of the genetic and environmental influences in hoarding symptoms, indicating that there is a strong genetic component to this condition.

Family studies, especially studies of twins diagnosed with obsessive-compulsive disorder (OCD) and Tourette syndrome, have yielded information about the familial patterns of hoarding. In particular, there is a now well-established body of science that suggests a relationship of hoarding among first-degree relatives. This means that if a mother or father in a family has a hoarding problem, their daughter or son is vulnerable to developing hoarding. This appears to be affected by gender according to one study where more female first-degree relatives (mothers and sisters) had hoarding symptoms compared to male relatives (fathers and brothers). More than

50% of those with HD reported that they had parents or siblings with the same problem, a much higher rate of hoarding in close relatives compared to people with OCD (30%) and community members who had no psychiatric condition (24%). These studies indicate that most people with serious hoarding problems are likely to have lived with family members who also have problems with saving and clutter. Accordingly, when talking with family members, it is important not to assume that the relative has no symptoms of hoarding.

Life experiences

There are many common misperceptions about the causes of hoarding that often refer to life circumstances such as downsizing a home or having too little space, financial hardship, or coping with an acute medical event or other physical limitation. While each of these situations (and many others) may make it hard to make decisions about getting rid of objects, none of them explain hoarding in and of themselves. That is, hoarding is not caused by any single life experience. Even the most difficult losses, such as the sudden death of a loved one or the destruction of home and property through a devastating fire or natural disaster, are unlikely to constitute the sole reason that someone develops a hoarding problem. Rather, hoarding appears to be due to multiple factors that may include traumatic events, as well as family and genetic history and psychological factors. The latter are discussed in detail in Chapter 6.

That said, people with HD do report more traumatic experiences in their lives compared to those without hoarding problems. However, one study of the co-occurring psychiatric conditions among people who hoard showed quite low rates of post-traumatic stress disorder (PTSD), a condition that can develop after very severe traumatic events like rape and war combat. That study was done on mainly middle-aged adults who were seeking treatment. But another study of older adults did find a link between hoarding behavior and traumatic loss (for example, of a partner or child) among those who developed hoarding late in life, especially when the hoarding began shortly after the event. This suggests that traumatic events (especially loss of loved ones) can trigger hoarding symptoms among vulnerable individuals under the right circumstances, but most cases of hoarding do not appear to be caused by trauma.

Why do people save stuff?

People who hoard save objects for almost exactly the same reasons that most people do—for sentimental reasons, because they are useful (instrumental saving), and because they seem beautiful or are aesthetically pleasing (intrinsic saving).

Sentimental attachment

Most of us save items because we associate them with special people, places, and/or experiences we have had. People who hoard typically save many more things for these reasons than most of us do, assigning special meaning to ordinary objects like an old list or a receipt or ticket stub, even if they are no longer readable. One difference between people who hoard and those who don't lies in the number and type of items they keep for sentimental reasons, and also the intensity of their attachment. For example, some people who hoard describe parting with almost any object as like "losing a piece of me." This strong sense of personal identity and/or emotional comfort ascribed to ordinary objects seems to extend well beyond what most people report feeling about their possessions.

Utility

Most people save things because they are useful. Like sentimental saving, the difference between those who hoard and those who don't lies in the type and range of items they consider useful and their conviction that it will in fact be needed. For example, in their 2010 book *Stuff*, Drs. Frost and Steketee described a woman who saved scores of cardboard tubes from toilet paper rolls because they might be useful for her son's art projects in school—but, in fact, she had no plan for how her son might use them and made no arrangements to achieve this goal. The items just sat piled in her kitchen with the *potential* to become useful.

Related to usefulness is a strong sense of responsibility for not wasting items. Many people with hoarding problems believe they have a responsibility to make sure that objects they own are not wasted and feel very guilty about discarding potentially useful items.

Aesthetics

Like the rest of us, people who hoard also save things they consider beautiful or aesthetically pleasing, and again, the difference lies in the number and types of items and intensity of feelings. For example, a person might keep all objects that are a favorite color or small scraps of paper or fabric to use in craft projects, even when the house is so stuffed that there is no space in the home to work on those projects. "Collections" is a term often used to justify saving multiple items that appeal to the person, as in the case of one woman who collected thousands of bottle caps in trash bags because she considered them "beautiful," although she made no effort to organize, catalog, or display them to others.

What emotions are associated with hoarding?

People who hoard save things because of immediate thoughts and personal beliefs or attitudes toward objects. Accompanying these thoughts and beliefs are strong emotions that range from very positive to very negative. Positive emotions are especially evident when people acquire new items, whether free or purchased ones, and when they come across items they already own but had forgotten about or been unable to find. These feelings include excitement, joy, pride, and hope. Such emotions often occur when the person thinks about the potential opportunities or usefulness of the items. For example, a man who fancies himself a "fixer" may become excited when he happens upon a pile of discarded tools by the trash bins in his apartment building. He gathers them up and takes them home, thinking about how useful the tools will be. The acquisition bolsters his pride in having tools consistent with his own identity as a competent repair person. Emotions of pleasure, satisfaction, and joy often accompany a decision to save an item. The object might provide a link to memories of enjoyable past experiences or simply be aesthetically pleasing. For example, a mother may experience joy in looking at a little sock her child wore when they came home from hospital, even though the sock is dirty and torn. Likewise, a father might be delighted to find a drawing of stick figures made by his 5-year-old son. These positive emotions are deeply reinforcing of acquiring and saving behaviors.

Especially prominent for people who hoard is the anxiety, worry, guilt, sadness, and even anger they experience when confronted with the decision about whether to keep or discard an item or whether to acquire something new. The intensity of these negative emotions can be so aversive that they will do whatever they can to avoid experiencing them. Some objects can elicit both positive and negative emotions. For example, a woman with a hoarding problem enters a thrift store and sees a set of eight depression-era water glasses. Immediately her excitement blossoms as she realizes they are a perfect complement to a set of wine glasses she already owns. She is giddy as she approaches the cash register, pays, and exits the store. During her bus ride home, she looks several times into the bag and smiles as she thinks of her good fortune at finding the glasses, even if the price was higher than she wanted to pay. As she enters her home after shopping, she is immediately overwhelmed by the sight of her too full house and the stuff she has already purchased and kept. She feels guilty for spending money on something she didn't actually need and remorse for bringing new things home when she doesn't have adequate space for the things already there.

What other problems commonly co-occur with hoarding?

Chapter 1 described various mental health problems that might account for what appears to be HD but in fact is due to another condition (for example, OCD, psychosis, or brain injury). Those conditions must be distinguished from hoarding to ensure that interventions are not mistakenly targeted at the wrong problem. It is also important to understand what sorts of psychiatric and other problems often accompany hoarding—these are the co-occurring conditions. In fact, it is rare for serious hoarding symptoms to occur by themselves. They are almost always accompanied by other mental and physical problems. Below we describe several of the most common ones, including depression, social anxiety, generalized anxiety disorder (GAD), and attention-deficit/hyperactivity disorder (ADHD).

Given the degree of distress and dysfunction associated with HD, it is not surprising that about half of people with HD suffer from major depressive disorder (MDD), a serious form of depression characterized by lengthy periods of low mood and loss of interest or pleasure in daily activities. For some, the depressed mood is less severe but still chronic and is diagnosed as "dysthymia." Depression tends to vary with the hoarding symptoms so that people with severe hoarding are likely to feel more depressed. That is, it is essentially a side effect of the debilitation due to HD and should resolve successfully following effective intervention for the hoarding behavior. Note that in some cases, the apparent accumulation of clutter follows and is directly attributable to severe depression and the person is not especially attached to their objects.

As noted in Chapter 1, in such cases a mental health clinician should consider a diagnosis of MDD rather than HD.

Approximately 25% of those who are diagnosed with HD also experience social anxiety that interferes with their functioning and leads them to avoid social situations. It is not surprising that people who live in hoarded homes are too embarrassed to invite other people into their home, and those who suffer from social anxiety are probably even less likely to do so. Interestingly, about 20% of people who seek treatment for social anxiety also have significant hoarding symptoms that they didn't mention when seeking help. No doubt hoarding problems provoke social discomfort and perhaps lead to social anxiety in some people, although it is also possible that people who are socially anxious may be prone to develop hoarding behaviors if they avoid social contact. It is also possible that both conditions derive from other family, cultural, or life experiences.

GAD, another anxiety condition, occurs in about a quarter to a third of people with HD. This problem is characterized by chronic worry about a variety of daily concerns. As noted above for social anxiety, nearly 30% of people who sought help for GAD at a psychology clinic also had hoarding problems but did not report them. Unfortunately, the connection between GAD and hoarding has not been explored.

The early research on hoarding presumed that it was one of several forms of OCD, but it is now clear that this is not the case. However, OCD does occur at much higher rates—about 18%—among people with HD than in the general population, where the prevalence is only about 2%. Co-occurring HD and OCD can be especially challenging to treat as both problems require specialized intervention strategies and it is not always clear how best to implement them in tandem.

ADHD also occurs in 20% to 30% of people diagnosed with HD. ADHD is characterized by problems with inattention and impulsivity or hyperactivity that began in childhood. It is the attention-deficit symptoms that characterize people with hoarding problems rather than hyperactivity. This makes sense in light of the disorganized clutter and other cognitive problems associated with hoarding.

Other psychiatric disorders can co-occur with hoarding problems, but generally these are diagnosed infrequently, at rates of less than 10%. Examples include bipolar disorder, panic disorder agoraphobia, specific phobia, and PTSD. Information about the frequency of psychosis and hoarding is not available as most research studies have excluded individuals with these problems.

Focus on: common features of hoarding

Hoarding is a complex problem that has been reported since ancient times. It is surprisingly common, affecting 2% to 6% of the general population in industrialized nations. Accordingly, most people know at least one person who has this problem. Several factors are associated with having or developing hoarding problems, including older age, limited income, and having first-degree family members who hoard. Traumatic life experiences may exacerbate hoarding tendencies, but few people with this problem suffer from PTSD. Hoarding of objects is fueled by the beliefs people have about acquiring and saving plus strong positive and negative emotions that accompany and reinforce the behavior. Commonly co-occurring mental health problems include depression, social anxiety, generalized worry, and attention-deficit problems.

3

WHAT ARE
THE NEUROCOGNITIVE
FEATURES OF HOARDING?

What do we know about brain patterns in hoarding?

In this chapter, the word *neurocognitive* refers to two aspects of the brain—neurological functioning and how the brain processes information, both of which appear to be affected in people who hoard objects. Neurological functions pertain to the chemical and structural pathways in the brain. Cognitive processing refers to perception, concentration, and memory, as well as comprehension or understanding.

Hoarding is defined by problems with excessive acquiring and saving due to difficulty parting with ordinary objects. These behaviors result in undue amounts of clutter that interfere with use of the home. The acquiring, saving, and clutter interfere with functioning and cause distress to the person who hoards and to others around them. It is important to be clear that hoarding is not the result of laziness or a character flaw. It is not the "fault" of the person who hoards but rather the result of thinking, emotions, and behaviors that become entrenched. Like most mental health problems, the symptoms develop slowly and are very difficult to control once the thinking, feeling, and actions are established.

Underlying the symptoms of hoarding are brain patterns that scientists are only beginning to understand. This chapter examines findings from brain imaging scans to investigate whether the brains of people who hoard appear to be different in some way. We will also look at what is known so far about how the brain works that contributes to the development and persistence of hoarding symptoms. Finally, the chapter considers beliefs and thinking patterns, the "cognitive factors," that contribute to hoarding problems. Some of this information will be useful in developing theories about hoarding (see Chapter 6) and ways to intervene effectively (see Chapter 7).

What do brain scans show?

Only a few studies have examined images of the brains of people who hoard using a technique known as functional magnetic resonance imaging, or fMRI. This work has been led by Dr. David Tolin. In their first study, Dr. Tolin's group asked a small sample of people with hoarding problems and another sample without these problems to decide whether to keep or discard a piece of mail they had brought from home. They were also asked to make other ordinary decisions that were not related to saving objects to see if the hoarding decisions produced different images than the ordinary non-hoarding decisions. Multiple images of their brains were taken in the MRI scanner during this process. Interestingly, the brain activity of those with hoarding problems was different from those without hoarding. Especially interesting was the brain activity in the frontal and temporal lobes that are involved in making judgments about the importance of situations. Activity in these brain regions was lower in people with hoarding compared to the non-hoarding group while they made ordinary decisions, but when they made decisions about keeping or discarding their own possessions (mail from home), these regions were overactive compared to the other group.

What do these findings mean? We suspect that people with hoarding disorder (HD) do not recognize a number of important things in their lives. For example, when acquiring something new or considering discarding something they don't really need (or perhaps even want), they don't seem to account for the broader consequences of their choice. This may also mean that people who hoard don't pay attention to their unpleasant cluttered surroundings, whereas other people find them intolerable. They may not actually "see" their homes as impaired unless someone calls their attention to important features they overlook. Their frontal and temporal lobes simply do not send the same messages that most people receive. On the flip side, when they are considering objects they own, the frontal and temporal lobes are overactive, calling more attention to things like junk mail than those items actually warrant. Presuming that this brain overactivity applies to most of their possessions, it makes the decision to discard any item much more difficult because everything seems important in some way.

As Dr. Tolin and colleagues point out in their book *Buried in Treasures*, biology is not destiny. Even if the brains of people who hoard have some abnormal patterns, this does not prevent people from changing those patterns, although it will entail significant effort to shift the focus of attention to important values and goals. As one woman noted, "Whenever I have to make a decision about whether to keep something, I ask myself whether having it is more important than having my ideal home." This strategy enabled her to discard much more easily as she persisted in applying her newfound rules about what was most important in her everyday life. In fact, another study by Dr. Tolin's group showed that people who had a good response to cognitive and behavioral treatment for HD showed more normal brain functioning after treatment compared to before. This suggests that changing one's behavior and thinking may actually also change the brain, a finding that has also been reported for other problems like obsessive-compulsive disorder.

How does the brain process information?

In addition to brain scan research, scientists have also conducted cognitive processing studies of various aspects of brain functioning, especially executive functioning skills, for people with and without hoarding problems. Executive functioning refers to a set of internal brain processes that enable people to manage their own actions and resources in order to achieve a goal. It is an umbrella term for the neurologically based skills involving mental control and self-regulation. Included in this group are the ability to pay attention; to organize, prioritize, and plan ahead; to start tasks and stay focused to complete them; to remember; to think flexibly and consider other points of view; to control impulses and emotions; and to keep track of what's being done. It's clear that executive functioning skills are essential for most ordinary daily life activities. Several of these skill areas have been studied in relation to hoarding, especially in the areas of attention, organization and categorization, memory, and decision making. It is important to note that most of the research in this area has been published only in the past dozen years or so. The methods used also differ across studies, so it is not surprising that findings are not always in agreement. Research on these topics is ongoing in several different laboratories, so the information in this chapter reflects current knowledge that is likely to increase in the coming years.

Attention

It is clear from studies of co-occurring problems in HD that many people also have difficulty paying attention and staying on task. In their seminal 1996 study, Drs. Frost and Hartl noted that those with hoarding problems also spontaneously complained of difficulty sustaining attention and procrastination. Attention refers to the ability to filter out distractions and is essential for successfully completing ordinary daily activities. People who hoard are easily distracted by things going on around them and by their own internal thoughts and feelings that can divert their concentration. As noted in Chapter 2, some people who hoard can be diagnosed with attention-deficit/hyperactivity disorder (ADHD), especially showing problems with attention more than hyperactivity. Even if they don't meet full diagnostic criteria for ADHD, people who hoard may still have problems with attention, especially when trying to make decisions in their own hoarded environment and when they are tired or in a depressed or anxious mood. Whatever the degree of difficulty, problems paying attention and distractibility interfere with a person's capacity to focus on sorting and making decisions about their possessions.

Prevalence studies have linked hoarding to ADHD. Other types of research studies also show that people with hoarding problems have more difficulty with attention than people without hoarding. However, this research does not yet make it clear whether ADHD and hoarding are related disorders or simply share some executive functioning problems. Some laboratory studies have been done to test people's ability to focus their attention and then repeat back information from memory. These studies have generally found no differences between people who hoard and other groups. Some preliminary research has examined simple visual attention and spatial memory, but those results are conflicting at this point. In any case, verbal attention alone does not appear to be a major problem for people who hoard.

Another nearly opposite problem is sometimes evident in people with HD whose attention can become hyperfocused to the point that they cannot stop thinking about an object and the reasons for acquiring or saving it. In these situations, they also have difficulty with flexible thinking and considering other perspectives that might allow them to decide not to acquire a new item or to part with possessions they don't need or want in their home. Paying attention in order to stay on task becomes an important part of the intervention process as described in Chapter 7.

Organizing and categorizing

Most people who don't have hoarding problems come up with a few main categories when deciding where to put objects in their home. Examples of categories are office supplies, books, clothing, kitchen utensils, and food. Within these categories, most people create a limited number of subcategories. For example, office supplies might be separated into writing utensils (pens and pencils), miscellaneous office tools and equipment (stapler, ruler), paper supplies (printer paper, sticky notes, envelopes), and paper files (banking, housing, medical insurance). This effort requires the ability to group similar items together and to organize them so they can be easily located. Some research suggests that people with hoarding problems struggle to accomplish these goals because they lack the necessary organizing and categorizing skills compared to their non-hoarding counterparts. When asked to sort their own objects into categories, they take more time and they feel more anxiety than people who don't hoard. They also tend to create many groupings with only a few items in each one, as if each item is so special that it can't be combined with other things. Of course, creating too many categories makes it very difficult to keep an organized home because groupings of similar types of items are needed so they can be found easily in the spatial storage within homes (cupboards, drawers, shelves).

Interestingly, the problem of creating too many categories only occurred when people who hoard were asked to sort their own items—it was not evident when they sorted other people's things. It seems likely that their thoughts and feelings about the value and usefulness of their personal items interfered with their organizing and categorizing skills, causing them to process information differently. In fact, most hoarded homes seem to be organized visually rather than practically. Dwellers are reluctant to put items out of sight—"out of sight, out of mind," as the old adage goes. Many, though not all, are able to locate specific information items among the many piles around them, suggesting that people who hoard do have good spatial memory (see below). Practice organizing their personal items is likely to be required in order for people with hoarding problems to return their homes to comfortable living spaces that can be used as they choose.

Memory

Many people who hoard indicate that they have trouble remembering what they need to do—chores, financial tasks, appointments, plans they've made. They tend to rely on visual cues to jog their memories, often to the point of so many visual reminders lying about (sometimes a veritable blizzard of sticky notes) that it is difficult to keep important agendas in mind. This is especially problematic if the visual reminders are not organized in any way. Accordingly, the problem with organizing and sorting interacts with concerns about memory. Some people make lists as memory aids, but when these are misplaced, they are obviously not helpful.

Research studies indicate that people who hoard express stronger beliefs about the importance of remembering information and show less confidence in their memories, as well as greater reliance on visual cues as memory strategies. Interestingly, scientific findings have been quite mixed so that overall, the studies of adults with hoarding generally haven't supported the idea that they have more verbal or visual memory problems compared to people without hoarding problems. However, a recent careful study reported that adults with HD were more impaired in visual areas compared to those who don't hoard. Problems with visual memory (the ability to remember visual images) appeared in 24% of those with HD, and about 30% had problems categorizing visual information such as images or written words. The researchers did not encounter problems with other aspects of executive functioning such as the ability to plan, process information, or pay attention. The researchers wondered if the frequent visual memory and categorization problems might be core features of the executive functioning problems that lead to difficulty processing, cataloging, and remembering where objects are placed, leading to a disorganized and cluttered home. Interestingly, these HD participants also demonstrated strengths in both verbal (comprehension and understanding) and visual reasoning (manipulating an image for understanding) ability compared to the control group. Perhaps people who hoard and experience problems in the visual processing area of the brain try to compensate for this by using skills in reasoning.

Regardless of whether people who hoard have actual visual or verbal memory problems, it is clear they have less confidence in their memories, expressing fears of making mistakes and forgetting important things. Of course, the cluttered environment almost guarantees they will forget some important things because they have failed to organize and separate important from unimportant items in their home. The absence of differences in memory for those with hoarding problems compared to other groups has been demonstrated mainly with middle-aged and younger adults. These findings may not apply to older adults whose cognitive capacity is declining and some memory problems (but not dementia) may be evident. With regard to treatment strategies for those without obvious memory problems, helping reduce anxiety while focusing on organizing skills that will enable them to rely on their memory is likely to be most helpful for those who lack confidence in their memories. As Dr. Catherine Ayers has indicated in her studies of hoarding in older adults, memory aids may be important, along with helping them develop planning skills to accomplish everyday tasks.

Decision making

Decision-making difficulties are considered by some scientists to be a hallmark feature of HD. The diagnostic criteria focus on difficulty discarding or parting with possessions, which can be considered a direct result of problems with making decisions about whether to keep or let go of owned objects. In their seminal paper defining hoarding, Drs. Frost and Hartl suggested that the fear of making mistakes made it hard for people with hoarding to decide whether to discard an object. Perfectionism also contributes as people weighed the pros and cons of possible future need and the consequences of making a mistake, hoping to make the right decision. Depression can also influence decision making as low mood tends to make ordinary decisions difficult to process. Self-report studies of decision making confirm that greater hoarding severity worsens decision making, and that people who hoard have more problems making decisions than those who don't hoard. Some researchers have also examined what happens in practical tasks that require them to make decisions. In the study of fMRI brain imaging mentioned earlier, people with HD took longer to make decisions and felt more anxious than their non-hoarding control group.

The decision-making problems appear to occur mainly in the context of choices about personal objects. However, for some people, other types of decisions are also difficult—what to eat, what to wear, who to call, where to go, and so forth. Perhaps they lack confidence in their choices and/or struggle with how to weigh the choices, unable to determine which aspects of a decision are more important than others. Lack of confidence may be caused by distress due to anxiety, depression, or problems with perfectionistic thinking, whereas difficulty weighing choices may reflect the executive functioning problems noted above. Regardless of the source of the problems with making decisions, effective treatment will need to help people practice making decisions about objects while they consider what matters most to them as they evaluate their choices.

Avoiding risk

Avoidance of risk is illustrated in the case of a man who saved items he thought he would need in case of an earthquake. He took great pains to acquire and save all sorts of preparedness items, ranging from sleeping and cooking needs to various kinds of survival and first-aid gear. Scientists have studied such avoidance of risk behaviors in hoarding using laboratory tasks that involve gambling strategies (although no money is usually involved). These tasks test a person's ability to respond flexibly, to generate solutions to novel problems, and to balance immediate rewards against longer-term negative consequences. Interestingly, people with hoarding problems did not respond differently than other groups, perhaps because their cautious efforts to avoid taking risks led them to perform well on the gambling tasks. The study of risk avoidance might need to examine behaviors in non-gambling situations to more accurately capture the types of risky situations feared by people who hoard.

Impulsivity

Impulsivity refers to actions in which the person does not exercise control over their cognitive and behavioral reactions to emotions. Sometimes impulsivity is categorized as hyperactive behaviors, like blurting out answers or interrupting others. Impulsivity figures prominently in problems such as compulsive shopping or gambling or substance addictions in which the person seems unable to resist urges to engage in behaviors that are immediately rewarding but ultimately quite harmful to themselves or others. Some studies show that as many as 80% of people with HD also meet criteria for an impulse control disorder, although these findings need to be confirmed in larger, well-defined samples. Laboratory studies of impulsive behaviors have shown mixed results, with some studies finding more impulsive actions among those with HD whereas other studies do not. Sensitivity to rewards is related to impulsivity and has been studied mainly in conjunction with compulsive buying rather than hoarding disorder per se. Intriguing findings from one study suggest that acquisition may be associated with susceptibility to reward while difficulty discarding is related to susceptibility to punishment. However, so far research on reward and hoarding is limited and the findings are inconsistent.

Problem solving

Because there is very little research in this area, we will focus this section on clinical observations in people with HD. Many people who hoard appear to have difficulty solving everyday problems, such as where to store things, how to remove large items that are too big for them to carry, how to fix broken things, and how to plan an event or a trip. For such everyday challenges, most people follow a series of steps in their mind to plan what to do and then carry out the actions. This involves various executive functioning skills described earlier, including planning, thinking flexibly, paying attention, and keeping track of progress. For example, when an appliance breaks in one of our homes, we might take the following steps:

1. *Define the problem.* We would first clarify the problem by looking at the appliance to determine what might be wrong with it and whether we can fix it ourselves or need professional help.
2. *Generate possible solutions and choose one.* This requires thinking flexibly and considering various options. All possible ideas can be considered at this stage of the problem-solving process. For example, we might (1) decide to try to fix it ourselves, using the internet as a guide; (2) call the upstairs neighbor and ask them to fix it because we know they have the tools and skills; (3) call and make an appointment with a suitable repair person; (4) decide that the appliance is too old and broken and throw it out. After careful consideration of the pros and cons of each possible solution, we can then proceed to step #3.

3. *Implement the solution.* We take action, such as calling the repair company/person to find out if and how repairs are done, whether our appliance is under warranty, and the cost of repair. If the call produces a plan that seems reasonable, we must then arrange to take the appliance to a shop or schedule a repair visit to the home.
4. *Evaluate the outcome.* If our plan works, we have solved the problem! But if it doesn't, we can repeat steps #2 and #3 to come up with a different solution and action plan.

None of these tasks are necessarily difficult in and of themselves, but they need to be done sequentially to accomplish the ultimate goal of having a working appliance. Those with HD often struggle to figure out what to do first, next, and so forth, and then to keep their attention focused on each step of the plan.

Do people who hoard have special thoughts and beliefs?

Among the important elements of cognitive functioning are the beliefs and attitudes people hold about themselves, about other people, and about their environment (the world and their role within it). Cognitive therapy, developed by Dr. Aaron Beck and others, is based on assumptions and research findings that how people think and what they believe influences their emotions and their behaviors. In addition to information-processing problems discussed above, the model for understanding hoarding put forth by Drs. Frost and Hartl (see Chapter 6) included mistaken beliefs about the meaning of possessions. They proposed three main types of beliefs that underlie hoarding behavior: (1) the need to control possessions (including discomfort with other people touching their things), (2) responsibility for possessions (to meet a future need and prevent harm to the possession), and (3) the need for perfection (for example, the need to read every article before throwing out a newspaper).

Their research indicated that when faced with a decision to keep or discard a newspaper or magazine, hoarding participants reported reasons to save it (avoid discomfort, maintain control, responsibility to be prepared) but did not consider reasons to discard it (for example, not enough space, no longer current, not interesting). In subsequent research, scientists examined these and some additional areas of beliefs in an effort to measure their intensity and relationship to hoarding behavior. These included beliefs about emotional attachment, concerns about memory, control over possessions, and responsibility toward possessions. Researchers have also identified concerns about usefulness and waste as important factors behind excessive acquiring and saving. These hoarding-related beliefs are described further below.

Usefulness, waste, and responsibility

There is reasonably good evidence that beliefs about the usefulness of objects and the responsibility not to waste them are common motivators for acquiring and saving behaviors. Interestingly, even among young adults without hoarding who were participating in a laboratory acquiring and discarding task, those who acquired the most objects perceived them as more useful compared to those who did not acquire. Unfortunately, people who hoard often perceive usefulness that is a stretch of the imagination. For example, one woman hung on to a torn and dirty stuffed animal, declaring that it would be a good toy for a small child. She reluctantly gave up the notion when asked to consider whether her own grown daughter would want to give it to her daughter (the woman's grandchild). When she began to view the object through their eyes, she could consider how damaged the toy was, and she agreed it was not a suitable gift.

Another rationale for saving is a sense of inflated responsibility toward possessions ("I'm responsible for the well-being of this possession"), reflecting a wish to ensure that objects are used and treated well. In addition, some feel responsible for keeping things that other people might need or want ("I must save this for someone who might need it"), even in the absence of any clear idea of to whom and when it might be of use. This sense of responsibility may also underlie the saving of multiple items of the same type, for example dozens of shampoo bottles that were purchased on sale to ensure that the person never ran out. Such responsibility for objects frequently extends beyond personal items to items owned by others and even "found" object without owners, perhaps due to the strong emotional attachments described below.

Sentimental beliefs and emotional attachment to possessions

Hyper-sentimentality toward possessions has been proposed to play an important role in how hoarding develops and persists. The extent of this attachment to possessions is captured in examples such as "throwing this away would feel like abandoning a loved one" and "I see my belongings as extensions of myself. They are part of who I am." In a study of thoughts verbalized while making decisions to keep or discard items, people with lived experience of hoarding were twice as likely as their non-hoarding counterparts to make sentimental, nostalgic, or reminiscent statements about their own objects. Examples are "It means so much to me" and "I'd be lost without it."

In one study of attachment, participants were given a new object (a keychain) and asked to rate their feeling of attachment when they first received it and again one week later. Not surprisingly, those with hoarding-related beliefs and behaviors showed more immediate attachment to the keychain than those without these symptoms, and the degree of initial attachment was a strong predictor of how attached they felt a week later. Interestingly, ownership or possession of the item increased emotional attachment for everyone, regardless of their hoarding symptoms.

Anthropomorphism seems to be a special case of emotional attachment, reflecting beliefs that objects experience feelings, as if they were alive. For people who experience these beliefs, possessions are accorded human-like qualities (for example, "Don't throw that coat on the floor; you'll hurt it!"), and their attachment to the possessions can be as strong as their attachment to people. Some research has indicated that people who hoard may have difficulty forming and/or maintaining relationships with people. Surprisingly little research has been done on early attachment patterns and on current interpersonal attachments among people with hoarding problems, although this concept seems central to understanding their beliefs, emotions, and behaviors toward possessions.

Beliefs about safety and control over possessions are also common and seem to be related to the strong attachment evident among people with hoarding problems. Objects confer a sense of comfort and safety, as evident when Irene in *Stuff* said, "I had such a terrible week, I just wanted to come home and gather my treasures around me." Another woman described her piles of things as "my bunker" and said, "I want to crawl into my cocoon." Not surprisingly, most people who hoard want to control access to their things, reflected in one person's statement, "No one has the right to touch my things." Of course, such a wish to control access to personal possessions is also generally true for everyone, but those with hoarding problems appear to be especially sensitive about this issue.

Confidence in memory

The scientific findings reported above indicate that hoarding is not associated with problems in verbal or spatial memory, but those who hoard are often concerned that they do not have a good memory. They fear that they will not remember events or information unless they keep relevant reading material like newspapers and magazines. Accordingly, one self-report measure of hoarding beliefs, the Saving Cognitions Inventory, includes items such as "Saving this means I don't have to rely on my memory" and "If I don't leave this in sight, I'll forget it."

Creative thinking

Many people with hoarding problems are intelligent and creative, some seeming to fit the mold of "information junkies" because they love to read and gather interesting information. One man seemed almost addicted to attending lectures open to the community to be sure he heard current information that might not be reported in print. Many people who hoard are creative artists or artisans who collect materials that might be useful in their artistic efforts, even if they have not had space to engage in this work for many years. Sometimes creative thinking is part of the hoarding problem. As noted in *Buried in Treasures*, thoughts like "I bet I could fix this up" and "I could make all kinds of crafts or decorations from this" generate excitement but lead to collecting and saving without the space or time to complete the task. One man filled his basement with broken items he'd picked up on trash day because he wanted to repair them, but the space was so stuffed that this was impossible. As Dr. Tolin points out, for such creative thinkers, "The brain writes checks that the body can't cash" when hoarding interferes with actions generated by clever minds with many ideas.

Perfectionism

As mentioned earlier, perfectionistic thinking occurs commonly as people with hoarding problems struggle to meet their own high standards. This interferes with decision making, so many people are afraid to discard objects for fear they will make the wrong decision, even when such a mistake can be corrected easily. Sometimes this type of belief involves magical thinking such as, "If I throw this out, I'm certain to need it tomorrow," reflecting a belief that a person should always have on hand things that could possibly be needed in the future. Another example of perfectionistic thinking, in this case incompleteness, is evident in one woman's discomfort with getting rid of an old suitcase she no longer wanted because she couldn't find the key and hated to throw it out without its key.

Is hoarding associated with emotion regulation?

The literature on HD indicates that emotional attachment to possessions is characteristic of people who hoard, along with strong negative emotions about parting with the objects. However, it is not very clear what drives these emotions. Some studies have found that people with HD have anxiety sensitivity, meaning that they become anxious easily, perhaps especially about loss of possessions. It is also possible that people who hoard tend to have difficulty regulating their emotions in general, reacting more strongly to challenging situations than others might. So far, there is limited research to support this notion.

Focus on: neurocognitive features of hoarding

Brain imaging studies suggest that people who hoard show different patterns of activation in the brain compared to people who do not hoard, especially in the frontal and temporal lobes that are linked to executive functioning capacity. Brain scans show underactivity when making ordinary decisions but overactivity while making decisions about their own possessions. It is possible that people who hoard are impaired in everyday decision making but hyperfocused when deciding whether to discard their own items, but more research is needed to establish this preliminary finding. While there are considerably more scientific data about executive functioning and information processing and hoarding, often the findings are conflicting and therefore inconclusive. For the most part, scientists agree that hoarding is associated with difficulty paying attention and distractibility, as well as problems with organizing and categorizing objects and information. Many people who hoard lack confidence in their memories, leading them to save things that others would not, but whether there are actual problems with visual memory is not yet clear. Decision making about personal objects is impaired, but it is not clear whether this is true for other types of everyday decisions. Nor have researchers established whether impulsivity and sensitivity to rewards are typical of people who hoard. Problem-solving deficits have been little studied but commonly observed for those with hoarding problems.

Several types of beliefs have been associated with hoarding, including beliefs about usefulness, waste and responsibility, and strong sentimental attachments to possessions. Other beliefs concern comfort and safety, the need to control possessions, objects as having human-like characteristics, and perfectionism. More research is needed to establish how often people hold such beliefs and whether they are central to the problem of hoarding. Likewise, whether anxiety sensitivity and difficulty regulating emotions play a role in hoarding is unclear.

4

WHAT IS THE IMPACT OF HOARDING ON SUFFERERS, FAMILIES, AND COMMUNITIES?

What kinds of problems does hoarding cause?

Although hoarding leads to adverse effects that are apparent to others, the person with hoarding behavior is sometimes unable to recognize the problems caused by having a house too full of stuff. Even if they have insight into the difficulties, they may not acknowledge the full impact on themselves and others, owing to embarrassment and shame. It may be too overwhelming to accept how seriously multiple aspects of their lives are affected by the hoarding. Below we describe the day-to-day impairment that commonly occurs in the domains of (1) household maintenance and tenancy preservation, (2) employment and finances, (3) physical health, and (4) mental health.

Household maintenance and tenancy preservation

Hoarded homes become overwhelmed by objects, often to the point that whole rooms are inaccessible and the common activities of everyday life like preparing food, bathing, doing laundry, and socializing become nearly impossible. Under these conditions, the home becomes very uncomfortable for the person who is saving excessively and for the family members who live with them or visit regularly. For a family of four, the availability of only one chair and one small portion of a table for eating means that family members must take turns and cannot share mealtimes. When clutter has accumulated so that a child cannot find an open space to study or a spouse cannot cross the room without stumbling into piles, clearly family members cannot function effectively, nor can the person with hoarding problems. In a study of older adults who hoarded, social service workers reported that the clutter prevented the home dweller from moving about easily and in some cases was knee high or higher, requiring elderly clients to climb over piles to move about. One woman reported "swimming" over the clutter to reach other rooms. Nearly 70% of the participants were not able to use furniture like sofas or beds, and several people slept on couches or the floor because their beds were piled high with their possessions.

Hoarding makes it difficult to keep up with everyday cleaning and maintenance as even simple dusting and vacuuming become very challenging. In severely hoarded homes, routine maintenance is frequently deferred because spaces cannot easily be accessed for regular upkeep. Repairing a broken pipe under the kitchen sink requires access to the kitchen and to the space in front of the sink so the cupboard doors can be opened. Also, the area under the sink and the sink itself must be relatively free of clutter for the repair work to be completed. Clearing any one or all of these spaces may be so daunting that the work goes undone, rendering the kitchen sink unusable for weeks, months, or even years. Of course, even when the spaces could be cleaned and cleared, embarrassment often prevents people who hoard from making arrangements for badly needed repairs. This means that in severe cases, hoarded homes often lack working appliances like stoves, ovens, refrigerators, washers and dryers, and even sinks. In one study of 62 older adults with hoarding problems who were receiving social services, clutter in the home prevented food preparation in over half the clients, and more than 40% were unable to use their refrigerators, kitchen sink (42%), and bathtub (42%). Some couldn't use the bathroom sink (20%) or even the toilet (10%).

Homes with excessive clutter can develop serious problems with dust or mold, have pest infestations (such as bedbugs, cockroaches, mice), become structurally unsound due to the excessive weight of items, or be plagued by water damage that threatens the stability of ceilings, walls, and floors. These situations create real risks to the safety of the occupants and any adjacent neighbors. Although some of the people who hoard are able to objectively acknowledge the need to attend to the safety concerns created by hoarded conditions, shame and stigma commonly prevent them from informing those who need to know and asking for help to remediate problematic situations. Fear of others' reactions is a powerful motivator for staying silent—being subjected to scornful or disgusted looks and judgmental comments is a risk few people are willing to take. It is not surprising that among older adults with hoarding problems who were referred to a social service agency, only 3% were self-referred, whereas 73% were referred by another agency and 21% by neighbors.

In privately owned homes, unfortunately people who hoard can more easily hide their home conditions and avoid dealing with the problem, until a crisis situation requires immediate intervention. Residents living in rental properties or in public or social housing are subject to regular inspections of their living units. This greatly increases the likelihood that significant clutter will be discovered and reported. Although discovery usually means that necessary repairs are made and home conditions are improved, there is also a very real risk of legal sanctions, including the threat of eviction, because the hoarding behavior and resulting living conditions violate lease agreements. It has been reported that 8% of people who hoard have been threatened with eviction or evicted due to hoarding, and hoarding appears to be a serious risk factor for homelessness.

Clutter in the home can create potential harm that ranges from mild to life-threatening. Injury and even death have been reported following incidents when tall piles of clutter become avalanches that fall on the home dwellers. Perhaps the greatest threat to life and safety is fire. Fire hazards in hoarded environments are many. They include the storage of flammable materials such as clothing and paper (two of the most commonly hoarded items) near heating sources like stoves, hot water heaters, radiators, and heating elements. Other sources of fire are electrical outlets and older types of electrical cords that are overloaded or are being used inappropriately. In addition, ways to enter and exit to the home through windows and doors are blocked by accumulated possessions, making escape during a fire much more difficult than in an uncluttered home. Further, the high volume of combustible materials like newspapers and magazines in hoarded homes provides fuel for fires that burn hotter and faster in a hoarded home compared to an uncluttered home. A fire study conducted in Melbourne, Australia, determined that 24% of preventable fire fatalities occurred in hoarded homes, even though fires in hoarded homes accounted for less than 1% of all fires within the city. The same study reported that functioning smoke alarms in the home were missing in 72% of the incidences of hoarding-related fire, and excessive accumulation of objects impeded the firefighting efforts in 38% of cases.

Employment and finances

The dramatic consequences experienced by people who hoard extend beyond the dwelling itself. Hoarding is associated with significant financial problems. For example, obtaining and maintaining employment are considerable challenges and affect both the sufferer and the family. Most of what is known about the impact of hoarding on employment and finances comes from a large internet study that included more than 800 people with self-reported hoarding problems. About 60% of the sample was currently working and the rest were homemakers, retired, or unemployed or had other temporary reasons for not working. Approximately two-thirds (575 people) reported that they missed at least one work day every month, and the average number of days of missed work for the entire group was seven days per year. This is substantially more lost worktime than is reported by people who suffer from depression, anxiety, and substance use disorders.

People with hoarding problems at home also reported having cluttered work spaces and difficulty finding things they needed to carry out their work duties. Anecdotally, some clients with whom we have worked clinically described some of the executive functioning challenges discussed in Chapter 3. For them, difficulty with sustaining attention, decision making, and overly complex thinking that interfered with problem solving created significant barriers for them in completing work tasks, leading them to feel frustrated and dissatisfied with their work performance.

In addition, the presence of physical clutter in work spaces such as offices or cubicles may put employees with hoarding problems at risk for public ridicule, experiences of stigmatization, and disciplinary action, including being fired. In the internet study mentioned earlier, among those who met criteria for hoarding disorder, nearly 6% indicated that they had been fired because of their hoarding behavior. Of course, being fired and the consequent loss of steady income can be catastrophic if it interferes with meeting monthly financial obligations like timely payment of rent or mortgage and essential bills. Interestingly, 20% of the more than 800 people surveyed had not filed income tax returns in at least one of the last five previous years. The researchers did not determine why this might have happened, but it seems likely that at least part of the problem may be difficulty finding the important documents and getting organized to prepare and submit the tax forms. These tasks rely on the very executive functioning skills commonly impaired in people who hoard.

Physical health

People with lived experience of hoarding are more likely than the general population to report a broad range of chronic and serious medical concerns. Among them are autoimmune diseases like rheumatism, fibromyalgia, and lupus, as well as stroke, diabetes, arthritis, high blood pressure, and ulcers. People who hoard also have statistically higher body mass indices (BMI). Obesity and other co-occurring physical health limitations may influence a person's ability to carry out the physically demanding work of sorting and discarding that is required to reduce the overall clutter volume.

The health of people who hoard can also be at risk because of adverse conditions in the home, especially squalid or unsanitary conditions such as those described in Chapter 1. The presence of squalor creates risk for respiratory problems, for example cardiopulmonary disease (COPD) and asthma, as well as possible infection from insect or rodent infestations. Of course, the presence of extreme clutter, especially in walkways or on stairs, also produces conditions that are ripe for tripping and falling. Piles taller than three feet increase the potential for harm of falling debris; in some cases, avalanches of unstable piles of items can be very dangerous to small children, people with disabilities, and frail older adults who are living or moving about in hoarded homes.

As piles of intermingled items accumulate in hoarded environments, it is not uncommon for people to lose track of prescriptions or other medical supplies that they need for good health. For example, a person with significant hoarding problems who is also diagnosed with diabetes may not be compliant with their insulin injections because they cannot find fresh injection supplies and testing paraphernalia amid the many other items in the home. The health of people who hoard will be compromised if they cannot find their prescribed medications, if they don't have the necessary space to use their assistive devices such as walkers or continuous positive airway pressure (CPAP) machines for sleep, or if they cannot gain access to their kitchen to prepare nutritious meals.

Mental health

People diagnosed with hoarding disorder frequently have other primary mental health concerns, as we have described in Chapter 1. The most common include low mood and sadness that is characteristic of depression, and fear and worry that accompany a range of anxiety disorders (especially social phobia and generalized anxiety disorder). Significant problems with attention may also be evident. The symptoms of these co-occurring problems add layers of complication to a person's attempts to resolve their hoarding behavior.

Relatively little research has been conducted on the personality features of people who hoard. Clinical observation suggests that some personality features may contribute to hoarding behaviors or interfere with effective interventions. These can include paranoia, exemplified in mistrust of the intentions and efforts of others. However, keep in mind that such mistrust may stem from past intervention efforts that were not respectful of the person's need for autonomy in making decisions about their possessions. Other personality traits can include dependency, especially with regard to leaning on others to make decisions, and obsessive-compulsive personality, in which the person applies rigid rules to guide their everyday behaviors, causing interference in ordinary functioning. Occasionally, a generally chaotic presentation is evident as the person who hoards jumps from topic to topic during the clinical interview and their daily life appears to be highly disorganized. Efforts to intervene by clinicians and other professionals must take into account the person's personality style. Mental health professionals who are experienced with co-occurring psychiatric and personality problems are likely to be helpful in planning and carrying out the intervention.

Broader than any single psychiatric diagnosis or personal traits are the daily effects of chronic stress on the person's mental health caused by living in a hoarded environment. Most people who do not have a hoarding problem enjoy spending time in their home and find it a relaxing and self-affirming space. In contrast, people with lived experience of hoarding commonly describe their home as chaotic and uncomfortable, even overwhelming, and express the wish for a more "peaceful" and "serene" environment without clutter. The stress caused by living in a hoarded home can lead them to avoid the environment, spending more and more time outside the home, making it even less likely that they are able to work on the problem. The impact of prolonged stress related to the clutter and the fear of sanctions from authorities and/or scorn from neighbors may produce additional stress-related problems like interrupted sleep, headaches, muscle tension, loss of or increase in appetite, and stomach upset. These hoarding stress-related problems are likely to resolve with effective intervention, but clinicians and other intervention providers must consider how best to help the client with hoarding stay motivated to work on the clutter.

Does hoarding cause family and social problems?

A fairly large portion of people with hoarding live alone. In Chapter 2 we reported on marital status, noting that a larger proportion of people with hoarding problems had never married or were no longer married (divorced, widowed, separated) compared to the population as a whole. Not surprisingly, the severity of hoarding was significantly lower for those who were partnered than for those who were not. In some cases, this is undoubtedly due to the role played by others in the home who help keep the level of clutter under control.

On the flip side, many people who hoard share their living environment with others, most commonly family members, who experience daily the challenges associated with their loved one acquiring and saving too many things. Even if people who hoard do not share their living environment with a loved one, those living nearby are often aware of the problematic conditions in the home and have concerns for the individual's well-being as well as for themselves.

Family problems

Most family members of people who hoard, whether they live inside or outside the home, are motivated to help reduce the clutter, driven by feelings of surprise, concern, fear, sadness, embarrassment, and confusion. Efforts to help, however well intentioned, can lead to considerable interpersonal conflict unless carried out in a thoughtful manner that respectfully involves the loved one with hoarding. Partners, children, adult children, siblings, and extended family members who make suggestions about how to manage the acquiring and hoarding may be met with strong emotions that range from positive (gratitude, acceptance, joy, relief) to negative (resistance, defensiveness, anger, hostility). It is not uncommon for people who hoard to offer explanations for their behavior, including their rationale for acquiring and saving. Attempts by family members to challenge their reasoning may provoke hostility and conflict, sometimes repeatedly, and most commonly without a change in behavior.

A surprising number of partners, children, and other family members are able to tolerate the clutter and remain living in the home, often driven by love, empathy, and deep commitment. Some family members, many of whom are driven by these same factors, decide to leave, and in the case of partnered relationships, may even pursue separation or divorce. The health and safety hazards and risk for psychological harm by staying with a loved one who is hoarding can be profound. Children who grew up in a hoarded environment and did not have the option of deciding whether to stay or go can be especially critical and resentful. Their experience tells them that their parent valued possessions more than the needs of the children. Research findings suggest that the level of rejection among family and friends of people who hoard is high—in fact, higher than the rejection rate of family members of people diagnosed with a severe mental disorder like schizophrenia. This familial rebuffing is of course only one cause of the social isolation people who hoard often experience. Even if the person who is hoarding does want to repair their relationship with family members, they often lack the interpersonal skills necessary to do so. The combination of diminished relationship skills and rejection by family members creates a perfect storm—one that can fragment and even destroy family relationships.

Social problems

Findings from various studies indicate that people with serious hoarding problems often live socially isolated lives, living alone in up to half of cases. It is not clear whether this social isolation is a preference that predates the hoarding behavior or, at least in part, a reaction to hoarding. The public discourse about hoarding commonly conveys erroneous assumptions about hoarding, including framing it as something other than a mental health problem. News reports, TV shows, and other media writings sometimes portray hoarding behavior as a moral failing, with the corresponding notion that a little more effort, and a little less laziness, could resolve the situation easily and quickly. These portrayals are not only incorrect but perpetuate the social and societal stigma associated with hoarding. In turn, people with lived experience of hoarding typically feel ashamed and protect themselves from judgment and humiliation by retreating to their home, alone.

Some people who hoard live very socially connected lives, engaging with community organizations, volunteering for their favorite causes, pursuing hobbies, and meeting regularly with friends. In contrast, others live in isolation, separated from loved ones, friends, and the larger community. Severe problems like animal hoarding and the presence of squalor in the home (see Chapter 1) create conditions that are especially likely to foster social isolation. Social anxiety (see Chapter 2) is another potential source of fuel for social isolation. For example, a person who hoards may repeatedly refuse invitations to others' homes for meals or social engagements, worrying that they would be expected to invite others into their home. Fear about not being able to reciprocate can prevent the person from engaging with friends entirely.

The social disconnection experienced by people who hoard may also be driven by interpersonal conflict with family members, co-workers, neighbors, housing providers, and others. When the person with hoarding problems receives suggestions for how to avoid acquiring and to get rid of their clutter, the ensuing anger and mistrust can ignite arguments. These conflicts may be followed by a complete withdrawal, whereby the person who is hoarding refuses communication or connection of any kind. In their book *Digging Out*, Drs. Michael Tompkins and Tamara Hartl offer useful suggestions for minimizing family conflict, strategies that are likely to be useful with workplace colleagues and others outside the home. In situations where someone is avoiding a necessary interaction, for example with a housing provider who is attempting to conduct an annual inspection in order to extend tenancy, Tompkins and Hartl recommend motivational enhancement techniques (see Chapter 9). The harm reduction approaches discussed in Chapter 10 may be especially helpful.

Does hoarding cause problems for neighbors and communities?

As we've described, severe hoarding has the potential to generate situations of extreme risk for the person and their family. These threats extend to others, including neighbors and those living nearby in the community. Particularly in high-density housing situations such as apartment buildings, hoarding presents a complex environmental and public health problem. The multiple jeopardies of fire risk, infestations, and general degradation of the home described earlier have particular implications for those who share walls and floors and for the building as a whole. One profound example of this risk was the 2010 fire in a high-rise housing building in the city of Toronto. The fire started in a hoarded unit and resulted in extensive destruction to many units in the building as well as injury to 17 people, including 5 children and 3 firefighters.

While people have a right to live as they wish in the privacy of their own homes, high risk occurs and tension is inevitable when the dwelling is so overcrowded with belongings that public safety hangs in the balance. Communities have a legitimate interest in maintaining order and must consider the greater good for all citizens. The various health and safety concerns that emerge from hoarding situations are the province of a diverse group of human service and first responder professionals. Police, emergency medical personnel, and utility service employees are likely to be some of the first professionals to encounter hoarding within the home as they respond to emergency calls for service, sometimes in very risky situations. Public heath, sanitation, and building inspectors are the professional groups that receive and investigate nuisance complaints about untidy yards filled with trash and accumulations of items considered by others to be junk. Housing officials, including property managers and building maintenance and housing support staff, encounter hoarding most commonly during the inspection process or when investigating complaints filed by neighbors. Concerns about the well-being of specially protected groups such as older adults, children, and people with disabilities may trigger investigations by welfare protection organizations. Other professionals in the veterinary and animal welfare community, pest control sector, and legal and medical professions may also become involved as needed.

A number of communities have come to the conclusion that these multiple and diverse professional and disciplinary groups will be most effective if they work in a coordinated way to generate solutions and bring the most appropriate resources forward to assist the person who is hoarding. Public–private partnerships and coalitions known as community hoarding task forces and hoarding response teams have grown in popularity during the last decade, especially throughout North America. Hundreds of such organizations throughout North America have been documented, and more appear each year. The benefits of these collaborative partnerships and coordinated service delivery models are described in detail in *The Hoarding Handbook: A Guide for Human Service Professionals* and summarized in Chapter 10. While there are many practical challenges in establishing collaborative community intervention efforts to support people with lived experience of hoarding, the benefits of a combined and united effort include the judicious use of organizational resources, increased human and financial capacity for response, and thoughtful use of a wide network of expertise.

Undoubtedly, community response to hoarding is sometimes driven by the practical reality of the enormous financial costs that affect various sectors and systems. In one study of health departments in Massachusetts, researchers found that in 80% of hoarding cases several human service sector organizations were involved, and each case required multiple visits by health department staff. In the city of San Francisco, estimates indicated that hoarding costs to landlords and human service organizations exceeded $6 million in a single year. Additional figures indicate that in 1 of every 25 hoarding cases, protective service organizations remove children, elders, or pets following investigations that provoke serious concerns about welfare and well-being. Community studies about the impact of hoarding on the medical system indicate that hospital discharge planning staff fielded special-needs requests for people who could not return to a hoarded home due to their medical condition. In one study, the community nurse on the hoarding response team in Vancouver, British Columbia, made an average of four contacts with other service providers for each of the 69 hoarding clients admitted to their service.

In addition to these community concerns, some cases of hoarding are processed within the legal system. Most often, hoarding cases are adjudicated in housing courts, and animal welfare cases are handled within the criminal court system.

Focus on: the impact of hoarding

Hoarding adversely affects people at multiple levels, including individual, familial, social, and community sectors. At an individual level, a person who hoards may experience interference in maintaining their home (including housing stability), in employment and financial matters, and in both physical and mental health. Family members who live within and outside the hoarded home also experience negative physical and psychological effects of their loved one's behavior. Family discord and separation may result from repeated conflictual engagements. Withdrawal from social engagements and social isolation are common problems among people with severely cluttered homes. The impact of hoarding extends from private personal domains of life to the public sphere when hoarding poses a threat to neighbors and to the community, involving professionals from many disciplines, including fire and rescue, housing, public health, social service, animal welfare, and medicine. Coordinated, multidisciplinary community responses are aimed at minimizing this societal-level impact.

5

HOW SERIOUS IS
THE HOARDING PROBLEM?

How do I know when my saving is really a problem?

As we indicated in Chapter 2, hoarding is a chronic condition that is likely to worsen over time if left untreated. This initially private mental health problem can rapidly become a significant risk to the health and safety of the person hoarding and also to family members and neighbors. Careful assessment/measurement is necessary to determine the severity of the problem and decide on the most appropriate steps for intervention. The types of assessments presented here include standardized clinical measures used by mental health professionals, as well as community-based measures of hoarding often used by municipal authorities. These were developed by clinical and community researchers and most have been tested to determine whether they are reliable (they consistently measure the same thing over time and by different raters) and valid (they measure what is intended). These assessments are most commonly used to determine the nature and severity of the overall syndrome and the specific symptoms and effects of hoarding disorder (HD). While most of the measures were originally designed for use by mental health clinicians, these assessments can be completed by a range of professionals, including those working in mental health, medicine, housing, and social work, among others. Clinicians who want more detailed information about the measures discussed in this chapter are encouraged to review *Treatment for Hoarding Disorder: Therapist Guide* (2nd edition, 2014) by Drs. Steketee and Frost.

The hoarding assessments described below were designed to be completed by a professional service provider or by the person who has the hoarding problem as a self-report scale. Sometimes family members or other people in the environment can fill them out. Here is a short list of the measures and who can complete them:

- Hoarding Rating Scale (HRS)—clinician, self-report
- Saving Inventory-Revised (SI-R)—self-report
- Clutter Image Rating (CIR)—self-report, home visitors (clinician, community service professionals, family members)
- Activities of Daily Living-Hoarding (ADL-H)—self-report, clinician, social service and housing professionals, family members

Below are brief descriptions of each of these instruments. All of them are available on the Oxford University Press website (www.oup.com/hoarding) or through an online search.

Hoarding Rating Scale

This brief five-item measure captures the main features of hoarding that are required for an HD diagnosis, although additional questions must be asked in a clinical interview to verify the diagnosis. The HRS includes one question each for (1) amount of clutter, (2) difficulty discarding, (3) acquisition, (4) emotional distress, and (5) impairment in functioning. Each item is scored from 0 (no problem/not at all) to 8 (an extreme problem), and the scale includes descriptions of mild, moderate, and severe symptoms to help the rater decide which rating is most accurate. The HRS takes about 5 to 10 minutes to complete. It can help clarify which symptoms of hoarding are most problematic and gives an overall severity rating by summing all five ratings. People who receive a score of 4 (moderate) or higher on both clutter and difficulty discarding, plus a score of 4 or higher on *either* distress or impairment, are considered to have a clinical level of hoarding that is likely to qualify for an HD diagnosis. Some people score high on the impairment but not the distress item because they are not upset about their hoarding behavior, although other people around them are likely to be distressed.

The total HRS score (sum of all items) can range from 0 to 40. People without significant hoarding usually have total scores below 10, and those with mild hoarding symptoms might score in the 10 to 20 range. Average scores for people with severe hoarding symptoms range from 20 to 30 and those with the most serious problems score above 30. In research studies using the HRS, all five items were strongly related, indicating that those with high scores on one HRS item often had high scores on the other items. In addition, the HRS total scores easily distinguished people who hoard from those who didn't, and they were strongly associated with other established measures of hoarding behavior. The HRS can be completed by mental health professionals during an interview or as self-report questionnaire by hoarding sufferers. The HRS can be found through an online search.

Saving Inventory-Revised

The SI-R is another systematic way to assess the severity of hoarding symptoms and is widely used in research and in clinical treatment. It is a 23-item self-report measure containing three subscales that measure the main features of hoarding during the past week:

1. Difficulty Discarding (discomfort about removing possessions and clutter)
2. Clutter (amount of clutter and problems caused by clutter)
3. Acquiring (frequency of buying and acquisition of free things).

Examples of SI-R questions are "How much of your home does clutter prevent you from using?" and "How often do you avoid trying to discard possessions because it is too stressful or time consuming?"

The SI-R is a widely used measure of hoarding symptoms in research and clinical settings. It takes most clients only 5 to 10 minutes to complete, although some people who have difficulty making decisions may take longer. Each item is rated from 0 (never) to 4 (very often) so the total SI-R score can range from 0 to 52. A total score of 40 or higher typically indicates a clinically significant hoarding problem. For the subscales, a serious problem is indicated by a score of 15 on clutter, 16 on difficulty discarding, and 10 on acquisition. Research on the SI-R shows that it is very reliable across time and internally consistent (items measure similar constructs). Like the HRS, it is strongly related to other assessments of hoarding symptoms and can accurately distinguish people with a hoarding problem from those without one. The SI-R can be found through an online search.

The Child Saving Inventory (CSI) was developed based on the SI-R. So far, it is the only research-validated measure of hoarding for children. Parents or caregivers complete this 23-item scale, which has subscales for discarding, clutter, acquisition, and distress/impairment. It is available through the International OCD Foundation's website (/hoarding.iocdf. org).

Clutter Image Rating

The CIR is probably the most widely used instrument to assess clutter. It can be used by any visitor to the home, including hoarding sufferers, family members, and community professionals. This instrument uses photographs rather than words to measure the volume (severity) of the clutter in various rooms. The CIR comprises nine pictures of three different rooms of a typical home—the living room, bedroom, and kitchen. Other rooms (dining room, spare bedrooms, bathrooms, attic, garage) can be rated using the living room picture. The nine pictures for each of the three rooms range from 1 (no clutter) to 9 (extreme clutter). Clutter is rated by reviewing the nine photos and determining the CIR image that most closely represents the volume of clutter in a person's home. A score of 4 or greater indicates a clinically significant amount of clutter in the room. However, clutter alone does not indicate a diagnosis of HD (see Chapter 1), since HD requires not only clutter but also difficulty discarding and distress or impairment in functioning. These symptoms are measured better by the HRS and SI-R or by one of the formal diagnostic interview assessments described at the end of this chapter.

Two separate studies have confirmed that the CIR is reliable across different raters and over time and is a valid measure of actual clutter. That is, the CIR provided consistent results when it was used separately by a professional and a client to rate the client's home and also when it was used to rate clutter in the same home on two separate occasions separated by a few weeks. Clutter scores from the CIR are also strongly related to ratings of clutter using other measures of hoarding behavior. The CIR can be found through an online search.

Activities of Daily Living for Hoarding

The ADL-H is a 15-item questionnaire that helps determine how much difficulty a person experiences as they try to do ordinary daily activities like sleeping in their bed, bathing, and preparing meals. This measure is specific to hoarding symptoms and is not intended to measure interference in daily home activities caused by other problems like physical health limitations. Each item of the ADL-H uses a scale from 1 to 5 to measure the degree of difficulty in which 1 means "can do easily," 3 means "can do with moderate difficulty," and 5 means "unable to do." A sixth column allows the rater to indicate "not applicable" when a rating does not make sense for that person (for example, "use stove" would not apply if the person lives in a single room without a stove). An average score is calculated by summing all items (except those marked as "not applicable") and dividing by the total number of relevant items. A score of 3 indicates substantial difficulties carrying out these ordinary activities of daily life owing to accumulated clutter and hoarding problems.

The primary use of this measure is to help professionals understand and sufferers realize which daily activities are most affected by the hoarding problem. By extension, the ADL-H can help guide treatment planning in order to focus on the areas that matter most to improve the person's ability to function. The ADL-H can also provide information about the person's degree of insight when the measure is completed by a professional rater and also self-rated. A discrepancy between their scores may indicate that the person who is hoarding underestimates the interference in daily activities. The ensuing discussion of different ratings and personal goals can be helpful in the intervention process. The ADL-H has been tested in two large studies of people with hoarding who were both clinically diagnosed and self-identified. It showed excellent reliability and validity, including distinguishing people with hoarding from those with other problems. The ADL-H can be found through an online search.

Is my thinking problematic?

As discussed in Chapter 3, people with hoarding behavior are motivated to keep many (if not most) objects that come into their lives, leading to cluttered living environments and interference in everyday functioning. In addition to the well-validated measures described above for these symptomatic aspects of the hoarding problem, determining what thoughts and beliefs drive their collecting and saving behavior is important in understanding it and selecting appropriate intervention strategies.

The Saving Cognitions Inventory (SCI) is a 24-item self-report questionnaire that assesses the attitudes and beliefs of people when they are trying to discard their possessions. This instrument contains four subscales: (1) emotional attachment to objects, (2) belief about memory, (3) need for control over objects, and (3) responsibility for objects. Examples of SCI assessment items include, "Throwing away this possession is like throwing away a part of me" and "I am responsible for finding a use for this possession." Ratings from 1 to 7 are used for each item, with anchors of 1 "not at all," 4 "sometimes," and 7 "very much." People with hoarding are asked to rate the extent to which they had difficulty with these thoughts and beliefs while making decisions about whether to discard an object during the past week. SCI scores are calculated by summing all items within each of the four subscales, and the total score is determined by adding the scores for all items. For subscales, the average scores for clinically significant hoarding are 38 for emotional attachment, 20 for memory, 16 for control over possessions, and 22 for responsibility. Total scores of 95 and higher are associated with beliefs characteristic of a hoarding problem; however, remember that this measure does not assess actual hoarding symptoms or HD.

Researchers have reported good "internal reliability" of the SCI subscales (meaning that items within the subscale are closely related to each other), and each subscale can discriminate people with hoarding problems from community members and people diagnosed with obsessive-compulsive disorder. As for the measures of hoarding symptoms described above, the SCI and its subscales are strongly correlated with other measures of hoarding. The SCI can be found on the Oxford University Press website (www.oup.com/hoarding).

How do communities decide when hoarding is a problem?

So far in this chapter we've described measures that are commonly used in clinic settings for people seeking treatment.

These measures can be administered by a clinician or by the person with hoarding (self-report) to determine the severity of hoarding symptoms. However, studies conducted in the general community suggest that only a subset of people with serious hoarding behavior receive a formal diagnosis and seek help from mental health clinics. This means that there is a large segment of people with lived experience of hoarding who are discovered by community members and service providers. In those cases, determining the severity of hoarding rests in the hands of social workers, housing providers, protective service professionals, public health officials, community nurses, and others in the human services sector. In Chapter 4 we discuss the impact of hoarding within the community, and in Chapter 9 we discuss community-based interventions for hoarding. The foundation for this work is the proper identification of hoarding problems, which is best achieved through thorough, thoughtful assessment.

Community providers who are charged with understanding the severity and impact of hoarding have some special challenges and also some unique advantages. Their assessment of hoarding is prone to some degree of subjectivity, influenced by providers' personal and professional attitudes and experiences. For example, a community professional who keeps a very tidy and clean home may overestimate the severity of modest amounts of clutter in another person's home. One person's assessment of another's behavior and living environment is influenced by life experiences that include familial, cultural, and societal information and attitudes about cleanliness, orderliness, and notions of how much is enough. Layered on the personal is the discipline-specific professional orientation that guides assessment.

For example, housing inspectors are trained to identify risky conditions in the dwelling created by substandard conditions or disrepair. Their work is guided by specific laws and regulatory mandates. When assessing a home, the inspector is likely to focus primarily on the residence and secondarily on the implications for the occupant. Contrast this with the approach of a community health nurse who may enter the same apartment with a primary focus on the person's ability to move freely in the space without risk of falling, as well as the ability to safely prepare and store nutritious food. For these professionals, awareness and honest acknowledgment of both the personal and professional influences on their views about hoarding will be helpful in facilitating a consistent and reasonably objective assessment. Talking with colleagues, especially those who have different personal and professional orientations, may also help limit biases that contribute to inaccurate assessment and understanding of hoarding problems in individual clients.

One significant advantage that many community providers have over clinician assessors is their ability to make a home visit to see firsthand the extent of clutter and its impact on daily functioning. Clinical psychologists and social workers and other mental health providers are typically limited in their ability to work with clients outside their offices, including during the assessment phase. By the nature of their tasks and mandate, public health officials, protective service workers, and first responders, all of whom regularly encounter hoarding, do their work inside their clients' homes. Being in the environment facilitates a nuanced understanding of the clutter and its impact on daily life. Someone who sees their therapist only in the office might describe their bedroom as "having a lot of stuff, so much that I can't sleep in my bed." A child protective service worker who visits that same home will be able to observe that the bedroom is packed with so many piles of objects that no one can enter the room because the door does not open fully. The use of photographs is often a good alternative when the mental health provider or community service staff member cannot visit the home. Asking people to take photos of every room at home and bring them to the office as part of the assessment process provides direct information about clutter and also helps them see their spaces through the camera lens. Sometimes that's an eye-opening experience.

The value of cross-disciplinary approaches to hoarding (see Chapter 4) is that a more comprehensive understanding of the person in their hoarded environment can be shared when professionals with different service identities communicate with each other. Though each community provider may have specific goals in the assessment process, everyone, especially the person with lived experience of hoarding, benefits when different perspectives are respectfully shared to provide comprehensive information. To accomplish this, community providers can determine the severity of a hoarding situation using some of the assessments described above. They can also use discipline-specific assessments. For example, elder service providers who are assessing how clutter influences the life of an older adult may use measures unique to their professional orientation with the elderly that are not specific to hoarding.

Below we refer to assessment tools that are of particular relevance to community staff members in assessing the presence and impact of clutter. These tools may also be helpful to people with lived experience of hoarding, their family members, and professionals in clinical settings.

Hoarding Interview

When community providers visit the home and observe the physical space, they can gain an understanding of the causes and impact of the accumulated stuff by conducting a semistructured interview about hoarding with the person. If there is no opportunity to visit the home, this interview can be conducted in an office setting. Regardless of location, the Hoarding Interview is best completed in a conversational manner with the client, which is somewhat different in tone from the standardized diagnostic Structural Interview for Hoarding Disorder described at the end of this chapter. Rather, the Hoarding Interview is intended to help clinicians and other professionals establish a relationship with the client while inquiring about important aspects of their hoarding behaviors. The Hoarding Interview covers the following areas:

- Onset and duration of the hoarding problem
- Home environment and its contents (including squalid conditions if any)
- Thoughts and feelings expressed by the person with hoarding about their possessions
- Current acquiring behaviors (what is collected, when, and how)
- Reasons for saving the items commonly found in the home
- Strategies for organizing belongings
- Role of family and friends—their attitudes about the problem, degree of distress, helpfulness
- Threats (immediate and past) to health and safety caused by the accumulated objects
- Personal problems due to hoarding (for example, debt, legal problems, family conflict)
- Prior interventions or attempts to clear the clutter and the outcomes
- Personal goals and values as related to current and future use of the home.

Human services professionals have many constraints on their professional time due to high caseloads and multiple task demands. The time available to complete a Hoarding Interview, or a portion of it, will be determined by the goals for the home visit. A police officer may only inquire about one or two of the above items while a social worker may ask for detail on most or all of the items. The mandate of the professional discipline also influences how the interview is used. For example, a housing inspector is not likely to spend much time exploring a person's values and goals when that can be the focus of a social worker's interview. And finally, the nature of the visit also dictates the focus of the interview. If the primary purpose of a home visit is a child welfare investigation, limited attention can be given to the reasons for saving in favor of attention to the risks to children caused by the clutter. The Hoarding Interview can be found on the Oxford University Press website (www.oup.com/hoarding).

HOMES multidisciplinary risk assessment

The HOMES assessment was developed by the Massachusetts Statewide Steering Committee on Hoarding and is intended to help users identify specific areas of risk in hoarded homes. The HOMES is a deliberately brief checklist that can be completed in 5 to 10 minutes by anyone entering the home, regardless of professional training. This includes repair people, mental health clinicians, housing managers, and family members. Community providers use this checklist to identify problem areas caused by accumulated objects and to develop intervention plans. The five domains are *health*-related household conditions (cannot use bathtub/shower, garbage overflow, presence of pests), *obstacle*s to safe movement (unstable piles/avalanche risk), *mental state* of the person (confused, angry, anxious), *endangerment* of protected classes of people (children, elderly, disabled), and *structural safety* (caving walls, loose floorboards). The HOMES assessment deliberately avoids using a formal scoring system, though it has been modified by community services organizations to identify conditions that create high risk from their perspectives. This assessment also has questions to clarify the client's insight and their willingness and capacity to address their hoarding behavior. The HOMES assessment is available at the Tufts Veterinary Medicine website (vet.tufts.edu).

Home Environment Index

The 15-item Home Environment Index (HEI) questionnaire was developed to help raters determine the extent to which squalid conditions are present in the home. It can be completed by the person living in the home or by a professional. This assessment uses a 0 to 3 rating scale for each item, where 0 means no problem (no fire hazards, all dishes washed and put away, no odor), 1 indicates a slight risk created by the condition (some fire due to paper clutter), 2 reflects moderate risk (many unwashed dishes), and 3 refers to extreme conditions (many health hazards, strong odor throughout the home). All 15 items are summed to yield a total score. Potential scores range from 0 to 45, and a score of 20 or above warrants careful assessment and intervention planning. The HEI was tested on a large internet sample whose hoarding behaviors ranged from minimal to severe. The HEI was reliable and internally consistent (items were closely related to each other) and showed construct validity (it measured what is intended). It was also strongly related to other self-report measures of hoarding behavior, including the HRS. The HEI is available on the Oxford University Press website (www.oup.com/hoarding).

Community use of the Clutter Image Rating

Earlier we described the CIR and its usefulness for clinical assessment. This measure is also particularly helpful in community settings to determine the severity of clutter. Unlike self-report measures, the CIR is unique in that no reading skills are necessary. An individual whose primary language is not English or for whom there are literacy concerns can simply point to the photograph that most closely represents the amount of clutter in that room of their home. The CIR's convenience and ease of use make it an ideal choice for an initial evaluation of overall clutter severity. It helps practitioners decide which rooms are most affected by clutter, and it is easy to use to assess progress in reducing clutter over time. Our research and community practice work has made us aware that the CIR is regularly used by fire departments, emergency first responders, housing and public health professionals, the court system, and especially in cases of child/adult protection.

What other assessments can help determine the severity of hoarding?

In this chapter we've directed the reader to the most commonly used methods of measuring the severity of hoarding and assessing related features. These include self-report and clinician-administered tests that are applicable to research and practice contexts for clinical and community providers. We conclude by drawing attention to a few additional assessment instruments relevant to hoarding and squalor in case these are useful to readers in the course of their work on hoarding. These measures can be found through an online search. The first two are diagnostic instruments intended to determine the presence of HD.

- *Structured Interview for Hoarding Disorder (SIHD)* is based on the criteria for HD in the fifth edition of the American Psychiatric Association's *Diagnostic and Statistical Manual of Mental Disorders* (DSM-5). It contains questions about clutter, difficulty discarding, acquisition, distress, and interference and inquires about co-occurring mental and medical conditions in order to make a differential diagnosis. It is intended for use by trained clinicians and can be found through an internet search.
- *Diagnostic Interview for Anxiety, Mood, and OCD and Related Neuropsychiatric Disorders (DIAMOND)* is a promising semistructured diagnostic interview for DSM-5 disorders that includes a specific segment to identify HD and make a differential diagnosis.
- *UCLA Hoarding Severity Scale (UHSS)* is a 10-item semistructured interview that contains questions similar to the HRS described above and also includes assessment of indecisiveness, procrastination, perfectionism, and task completion rate. It is designed for use by mental health clinicians and can be found through an internet search.
- *Compulsive Acquisition Scale (CAS)* is an 18-item assessment to determine the presence of excessive acquisition.

The measure has two subscales: compulsive buying (12 items about the reasons for buying and interference caused) and acquisition of free things (6 items about picking up free things). The CAS can be used in clinical and community settings and is especially relevant for those with serious acquiring problems.

- *Environmental Cleanliness and Clutter Scale* was developed by Dr. John Snowden and colleagues to measure aspects of domestic squalor such as accumulation of items, cleanliness, and the presence of vermin. Individual items of this scale were also shown to be closely related. A score greater than 12 usually indicates moderate or severe squalor. It is available at projects.hsl.wisc.edu.

Focus on: measuring the severity of hoarding

Accurate assessment of the amount of clutter in the home, the degree to which it causes interference in functioning, and the beliefs and mechanisms that promote saving and make discarding difficult are all important aspects of hoarding symptoms, especially when developing effective interventions (see Chapters 7, 8, and 9). Standardized measures used by clinicians and human services providers in interview and self-report format in clinical and community settings are useful for both initial and ongoing assessment. The instruments and tools now widely available facilitate assessment of the features of hoarding, accumulation of clutter, the presence of squalor, and the impact of acquisition. Most assessments can be completed in a short time, and some are very brief, taking only 5 to 10 minutes. Numerical scales with anchor words facilitate completion of most of the assessments described in this chapter, although some people with hoarding problems can find the decision-making aspect of completing self-report measures challenging. Community assessment strategies are aligned with the roles of service professionals and facilitate an understanding of hoarding and its individual manifestations across various services.

6

WHY DO PEOPLE HOARD?

In previous chapters we've described the criteria for hoarding disorder (HD) and detailed the features of acquiring, saving, and clutter. We also discussed the common features associated with hoarding symptoms and HD, including demographic characteristics, as well as the beliefs, emotions, and behaviors, including brain activity and cognitive processes, that accompany these. How do we explain why these symptoms and features occur in combination?

Acquiring behaviors are in fact necessary for the survival of humans and some animals. Humans and animals need to procure food and shelter, and humans require clothing and a few other basic necessities. Saving enables humans to have such necessities available when required by environmental circumstances. In addition, for humans, acquisition and ownership are important for social and psychological functioning, for example in reflecting social status and role definition. People also rely on acquisitive behaviors like shopping for food and clothing as part of routine social and leisure activities. Keeping sentimental items like letters, photos, and travel mementos facilitates our recall of past experiences, displays our interests, and connects us to each other. In order to understand the development of excessive acquiring and saving and the resulting clutter, we need to consider both animal and human models that might explain these behaviors and guide intervention strategies.

In this chapter, we first point to a few biological and psychological features described in previous chapters that might contribute to hoarding but do not constitute full conceptual models. These include genetic features, mood states, and trauma. We then describe interesting animal models for hoarding and how these might apply to human animals as discussed by Dr. Stephanie Preston in her work on hoarding by animals and by Dr. Stephen Kellett in his "site security model" for humans. Finally, we summarize cognitive-behavioral models put forward by Drs. Randy Frost, Gail Steketee, and Michael Kyrios and their colleagues.

What features might help us understand how hoarding develops and persists?

Genetics

As noted in Chapter 2, genetic studies of hoarding indicate that hoarding runs in families and is readily inherited. In one study, genetic factors accounted for half of the hoarding presentation, and the rest was accounted for by environmental factors, especially for women. Researchers have also reported that both hoarding and indecisiveness occur commonly among relatives of people with hoarding. With high rates of hoarding evident in family members, any theories of hoarding must include genetic heritability as a vulnerability factor.

Mood

Negative mood and specifically depression are common features of HD and may be important in the development of hoarding symptoms. Besides depression, other negative emotional states include anxiety, grief, loss, sadness, guilt, frustration, confusion, anger, and suspiciousness. These types of feelings are associated with the avoidance of discarding and can interfere with the person's ability to let go of unneeded and unwanted stuff. Negative mood can also lead to excessive buying to offset depressed feelings and improve one's mood while shopping or obtaining a new free item. As noted in the description of compulsive buying in Chapter 1, acquiring produces short-term relief from negative mood, which reinforces shopping as a coping strategy, but unfortunately it ultimately produces longer-term social, financial, and interpersonal difficulties and ultimately a negative mood. At the same time, acquiring and saving is also reinforced by positive emotions like excitement, joy, pleasure, satisfaction, and pride. This up-and-down mood pattern seems to resemble what takes place in some addictions (for example, gambling).

Trauma

Some research has also indicated that problematic hoarding is associated with personal histories of negative life events, and some degree of traumatic experiences. This is evident in studies showing that people with hoarding problems, especially those with more severe clutter in their home, are more likely to have had traumatic experiences than those without hoarding. In a large web-based study, about three-quarters of people with hoarding reported experiencing interpersonal violence in the past, and late-onset hoarding was associated with recent stressful life events. In another study, over half of those who hoarded connected the onset of their difficulties to stressful life environments, and this was less common among people whose hoarding began early in life. It is possible that traumatic life events play a greater role in adult-onset hoarding compared to early onset in children and adolescents. A history of traumatic events, perhaps especially losses, might predispose vulnerable people to derive greater comfort from the objects around them.

Can animal models help us understand human hoarding?

It is interesting to consider whether animal behavior might provide a model for understanding human hoarding. Both food hoarding and nesting seem analogous behaviors to human hoarding. Some scientists suggest that hoarding might reflect a "fixed action pattern" akin to the building of nests by mammals and birds. In a similar vein, human hoarding may be the modern-day equivalent of survival instincts from days of yore when both humans and animals competed for scarce resources. Dr. Stephanie Preston and her colleagues have studied hoarding behavior in various small mammals that are known to hoard food and occasionally objects.

The term "hoarding" in humans has different connotations than in non-human animals. In contrast to human hoarding, which is considered pathological behavior, in animals, hoarding refers to normal food-storing behaviors that enable various species to have food when it is in short supply due to weather variations or competition. In fact, normal human behavior also involves various forms of adaptive hoarding that is key to success and survival. That is, hoarding is an appropriate response to perceived shortages, uncertainty, or threat, is linked to physiological stress, and engages parts of the decision and reward systems of the brain (the mesolimbocortical system) that are needed to respond appropriately.

Hoarding behavior in animals, both rodents and birds, takes the form of food storage. These animals fall into two main types: scatter hoarders and larder hoarders. Some scatter-hoarding animals such as squirrels disperse seeds across their home range singly or in small caches they must remember over time. Other animals engage in larder hoarding, collecting all of their stored food in one location such as a burrow that they defend from competitors. Scatter hoarding is more costly with regard to time and effort required and the risk of predators, but it is required for those species that face more competition for food and/or are too small to defend their food from other animals. Scatter hoarding also requires special memory systems to recall the location of each cache. Larder hoarding takes less effort and is more common in species such as hamsters and rats that face less competition for resources and/or are larger or dominant enough to defend their larder against pilferage.

Humans exhibit both larder hoarding and scatter hoarding to adaptively allocate resources. Before modern conveniences were available, people stored their harvested food in a root cellar whose underground temperature stayed cold throughout the year. Stores of food were referred to as "larders." Like their animal counterparts, people worked to amass adequate stores of wood for cooking and heating as well as food to survive long cold winters in northern climates. Larder hoarding continues today to avoid starvation and death in the event of catastrophes, for example from earthquakes, major storms, and extreme cold. Refrigerators and freezers can be considered larder hoard sites where food is stored in one large space available for long-term access—it is less costly and safer than daily foraging for the items. Even money and valuables are kept in larders (bank vaults) to hold them for future use and hide them from potential thieves. In many homes, attics and garages are used to store seasonal items for future use. Scatter hoarding also occurs as some people keep special foods hidden around the house to control access to these resources (so others will "keep their paws off," as one woman put it). As in animals, scatter hoarding in humans requires greater spatial and prospective memory processes to avoid losing or forgetting the caches. Risk and reward strategies play a role in both animal hoarding and in human hoarding of money, which is both scattered and cached for immediate use and investment purposes.

Given that both animals and humans use hoarding methods for survival and everyday living, it is clear that hoarding itself is not inherently unusual and/or pathological in humans. One might also argue that clinically problematic hoarding is not necessarily distinct from everyday adaptive hoarding behavior since both maintain and protect resources that are considered valuable and important for future use. However, people with HD appear to lack sensitivity to the environmental context that non-human animals and most humans use when determining the value of objects and the associated risks. People with HD also exhibit both scatter hoarding and larder hoarding, although no direct study of these types of behaviors has been made. Most obvious is larder hoarding, as those with HD amass all items in a single location (the home), although some also store items in other locations (for example, storage units) when they have too much stuff to fit into their home. Cluttered homes appear similar to the burrows of larder-hoarding rodents as items that are perceived to be valuable, necessary, and important are amassed for potential future use. Like their hunter-gatherer ancestors, current-day humans with HD actively defend their stores from relatives and city officials trying to clear the debris, viewing their items as essential, like the food stores protected by animals. In addition, items that are removed are quickly replaced, ensuring that the supply remains constant, suggesting that maintaining the stockpile is more important than the specific items in it. Scatter hoarding is evident when the person fears that items will be taken and hides them in special locations. However, if this "instinctive" behavior is applied too often, scatter hoards are difficult to remember and retrieve, even when needed.

Another possible motivation for both normal and unhealthy hoarding behavior is the nesting instinct. Perhaps the collected goods of those with severe hoarding behaviors represent material protection from the outside world, representing nesting material that provides warmth and safety from predators. This fits the contents of many cluttered homes that include packing materials and even trash that has little future use but might be considered useful protective material. People with HD often report feeling safe with their items and vulnerable without them. Accordingly, the need to replenish lost stores could represent a nesting instinct more than protection of valued items. In such cases, internal emotional cues like anxious feelings would be expected to determine when a person acquired new materials if safety was the main concern. This motivation to acquire might explain the low insight of people with HD and also why individuals would persist in hoarding because their chronic insecurity would interfere with their ability to suppress the drive to hoard more items.

It seems likely that at least some cases of human hoarding reflect basic primal animal hoarding and nesting instincts, with different proportions evident across individuals. Dr. Preston suggests that modest levels of hoarding could reflect animal hoarding instincts that respond reasonably well to cognitive and behavioral interventions such as evaluating the costs and benefits of keeping items and learning to organize possessions (see Chapter 7). Severe hoarding more likely reflects a protective burrowing and nesting instinct that may be more difficult to treat without calming underlying fears and insecurity. Chapter 9, on community interventions, provides strategies for people with severe hoarding problems with low insight that might be based on such primal nesting instincts.

Is attachment to possessions related to problems with attachment to people?

Biological, psychological, and social models for psychiatric disorders assume that these conditions are multiply determined. That is, in addition to biological features in the animal behavior theories above and in genetic (Chapter 2) and brain structures (Chapter 3), there are also likely to be psychological and social influences on human behavior. Such models also focus on the thoughts, emotions, and behaviors and their interactions with biology and social experiences. Psychological models for hoarding also assume that serious hoarding problems are likely to be caused by multiple biological, psychological, and social factors. The biological conceptualization following animal behavior described above is a compelling one but probably not sufficient to explain all hoarding behavior, especially the social and cultural influences on hoarding and the symbolic emotional attachments to objects and other emotional components of hoarding often seen among affected individuals. Below we describe two models that focus on security needs and developmental attachment to help explain hoarding symptoms.

Site security model

Dr. Stephen Kellett has conceptualized hoarding as a security-based strategy in humans that follows directly from the animal research described above with regard to larder hoarding. This "secure site" model proposes that people with hoarding problems seek to secure their environment. Also evident in many animal species and early humans, such a goal has survival and breeding advantages. People who hoard see objects as resources and experience a sense of security from their acquiring and saving behaviors, forming strong attachments to their possessions, sometimes in place of interpersonal relationships. This seems to facilitate a sense of control over one's environment in the face of uncertainty about future needs or circumstances—that is, objects must be kept in case they might be needed some time in the future. They must also be kept in sight if possible, to reassure the person that they are still available and under the owner's control.

Handling the item seems to increase its perceived value as an exclusive resource, special and different from other objects. Attractive objects are of particular interest to people, and this has also been observed in animals. For example, laboratory rats seek out novel items with special visual and/or tactile features—for example, shiny or soft objects—even when they are not edible or otherwise useful. For humans, the sense of having enough items seems to be missing, perhaps because of chronic doubt and indecision often associated with hoarding. In the secure site model, it is suggested that although animals use larder hoarding to secure energy (from food), humans with hoarding seek insurance against anxiety about having enough. Concern about making mistakes by discarding an object that is later needed overwhelms the normal sense of what is "enough" in a larder hoard. Indecision and avoidance follow. As discussed below, adverse childhood events like deprivation and loss that disturb early crucial attachments are hypothesized to trigger later hoarding behaviors. Dr. Kellett proposes intervention strategies that follow from this model, especially efforts to change mistaken attitudes and beliefs so people can differentiate objects that serve as true resources from those that do not. These beliefs might be divided into fear themes and "just in case" themes to help people address anxiety about security and actual need for resources.

Identity and attachment model

Dr. Michael Kyrios and others have proposed cognitive, behavioral, and emotional models of hoarding that are based on concepts of self-identity. Their work integrates developmental and psychological concepts such as parenting, early attachment styles, and personality features. In this model, illustrated in Figure 6.1, an ambivalent sense of self-worth emerges from early childhood parenting and experiences in which parental criticism and rejection occur and are disguised under a veneer of devoted parenting. Those who grow up with such conflicting parental behaviors are thought to use various strategies to seek certainty, minimize threat, and protect themselves from criticism. The resulting perfectionistic and rigid behavior patterns only increase the person's vulnerability to anxiety, depression, and obsessive-compulsive symptoms. In support of these ideas, research on hoarding behavior indicates that uncertainty about parental attachment and ambivalence about oneself may be related to materialism, hoarding behavior, and compulsive buying. Also, people who hoard report feeling less warmth in their family compared to non-hoarding individuals, although not necessarily less than people with anxiety disorders. In a related vein, lack of warmth is associated with more severe hoarding. In one case study, people with hoarding

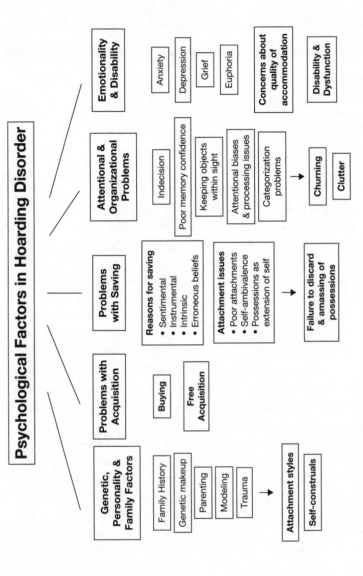

Figure 6.1. Dr. Michael Kyrios and Colleagues' Model for Hoarding Disorder

problems cited emotional and material deprivation in childhood and not being allowed to keep items as possible factors in their attachment to objects.

Related to this concept is the idea that possessions can increase feelings of security as symbols of interpersonal ties with others and cues for recalling past positive experiences. Hoarding is associated with hyper-sentimentality about personal belongings, such that people who hoard derived more comfort from their possessions than people who don't hoard. It is common to observe that people who hoard feel their possessions as extensions of themselves and feel responsible for taking care of the objects. Some anthropomorphize objects, assigning them human qualities and sometimes preferring them to humans. Others keep possessions to maintain a connection to their past (for example, loved ones who have died) or to compensate for a traumatic past. This has been called "object–affect fusion," meaning that objects are intertwined with emotions and become symbols the person cannot part with. Similar ideas have been proposed to explain why people hoard animals—that the animals provide vulnerable people with a sense of security that helps them avoid feelings of emptiness and depression. Their relationship to the animals is immature, meeting the needs of the person but not the animals, as those who hoard animals seem unaware of their poor health.

Overall, there is support for the idea that the strong attachment to objects in hoarding may stem from a compromised early childhood when attachment and self-identity patterns develop. These early developmental experiences trigger compensatory attachment to objects to defend the person from uncertainty and threat. The sense of responsibility toward objects, the need to exercise control over possessions, and the focus on maintaining strong memories about objects are consistent with such notions.

Is there a comprehensive psychological model that explains hoarding symptoms?

In addition to the biological models described above, a cognitive-behavioral model of hoarding was originally described by Drs. Frost and Hartl and updated by Drs. Frost, Steketee, and Kyrios. They propose that the primary symptoms of hoarding (acquisition, saving, and clutter) are caused by several different factors, as illustrated in Table 6.1 and Figure 6.2. This model includes concepts of vulnerabilities, including early attachment problems, information-processing problems, meanings and beliefs about possessions, positive and negative emotions, and resulting acquiring and saving behaviors. This model has been used extensively as the basis for advancing treatment of hoarding behaviors.

Vulnerability factors

Chief among the various personal and family vulnerability factors for hoarding are genetic predisposition, family history of hoarding, stressful and traumatic life experiences, and current negative mood (depression, anxiety). As noted in Kyrios's attachment model described earlier, among the adverse life experiences are events such as the loss of caretakers and unstable living situations that might predispose a person to develop attachments to possessions that evolve into hoarding problems. Likewise, the presence of serious depression, generalized anxiety, or social anxiety could contribute to difficulty making decisions and an excessive focus on objects to avoid people. In some cases, individuals might hold core beliefs that the world is a dangerous place and they must be prepared. It is unlikely that each person who hoards has the same vulnerabilities, but it is likely that all have some predisposing factors that set them up for hoarding symptoms. Understanding these will help with decisions about what treatments might work best and how to implement them.

Table 6.1. Elements that Contribute to Hoarding Problems of Acquiring, Saving, and Clutter

Basic Elements	Components	Examples
Personal and family vulnerabilities	Family history of hoarding	Hereditary traits, biological underpinnings
	Comorbid problems	Depressed mood, social anxiety, obsessive-compulsive symptoms, attention problems
	Parental values and behavior	Acquiring, difficulty discarding, clutter in the home, decision making, beliefs and values about waste, sentimentality
	Physical constraints	Health, time, household space
	Adverse life events	Loss of caregiver, moving, deprivation, assault
Information-processing problems	Attention	Difficulty sustaining attention on a difficult task
	Categorization	Problems grouping and organizing objects into categories
	Memory	Poor verbal or visual memory leading to reliance on visual cues
	Perception	Strong visual attraction to objects, failure to notice clutter
	Associative or complex thinking	Generates lots of ideas about or uses for objects, creative ideas, focus on nonessential details, inability to separate important from unimportant details
	Decision-making problems	Considering too many facets of a problem, ambivalence; may be related to fear of making mistakes

(continued)

Table 6.1. Continued

Basic Elements	Components	Examples
Meaning of possessions (reasons for saving)	Beauty	Finding beauty and aesthetic appeal in unusual objects
	Memory	Belief/fear that memories will be lost without objects or that objects contain or preserve memories
	Utility/opportunity/ uniqueness	Seeing the usefulness of virtually anything; seeing opportunities presented by objects that others don't
	Sentimental	Attaching emotional significance to objects; anthropomorphism
	Comfort/Safety	Perceiving objects (and related behaviors like shopping) as providing emotional comfort; objects as sources of safety (safety signals)
	Identity/validation of self-worth	Belief that objects are part of the person or represent who the person can become; objects as representation of self-worth
	Control	Concern that others will control one's possessions or behavior
	Mistakes	Perfectionistic concern about making mistakes or about the condition or use of possessions
	Responsibility/waste	Strong beliefs about using possessions responsibly, not wasting them, not polluting the environment
	Socializing	Buying or collecting items provides social contact not available in other ways

Table 6.1. Continued

Basic Elements	Components	Examples
Emotions	Positive	Excitement, joy, pleasure, comfort, satisfaction
	Negative	Anxiety, guilt, grief, sadness, anger
Learning processes	Positive reinforcement	Saving and acquiring produce positive emotions
	Negative reinforcement	Saving permits escape or avoidance of negative emotions
	Effects of hoarding behaviors	Prevent the opportunity to test current beliefs and develop alternate beliefs

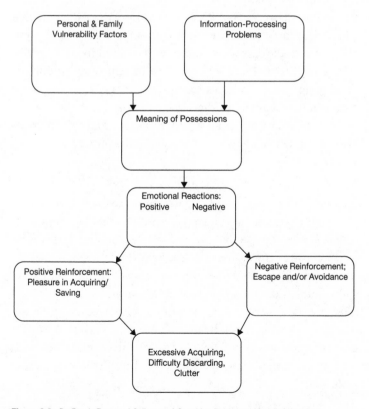

Figure 6.2. Dr. Randy Frost and Colleagues' Cognitive-Behavioral Model of Hoarding

Information-processing problems

Clutter in a hoarded home typically contains disorganized piles of possessions that are rarely kept in good condition. As noted in Chapter 3, the disorganization is thought to derive from compromised attention, categorization, and organizational abilities, especially for personal possessions, and possibly from memory problems but more likely from lack of confidence in memory. People with hoarding problems tend to focus on the unique properties of objects, making it difficult to make decisions about combining objects into similar groupings. Other cognitive features that contribute to hoarding include poor spatial attention, slow reaction times, impulsivity, and reliance on visual-spatial recall strategies rather than categorical ones, leading people to avoid putting things away. These limitations in cognitive processing reduce the person's capacity to sort and make decisions about possessions. The tendency to keep possessions in view plus attentional difficulty increases distractibility and leads to the churning of objects, producing clutter and disorganization. In any case, cognitive factors are certainly important in the development and persistence of hoarding behaviors, and strategies that can improve these are likely to be useful in resolving the problem.

Beliefs

Vulnerability factors and information-processing problems combine to confer special significance or meaning to possessions. For example, a daughter raised by a father whose motto was "waste not, want not" might believe that even broken or damaged objects should never be wasted. In this cognitive-behavioral model, the perceived value assigned to objects influences decisions to acquire and save possessions that are viewed as having special value. This can be (1) current or future instrumental or practical value, (2) sentimental value with strong emotional attachments, and (3) aesthetic or inherent value, as in works of art. All people report acquiring and saving things for these three reasons, but people who hoard assign more value to their objects and have stronger feelings of attraction and concerns about loss. People who hoard believe that objects help keep them safe and feel responsible for ensuring that objects are used and appreciated. They also fear being unable to remember events or information without object cues, and feel an intense need to control their possessions. Such beliefs increase excessive acquisition and also difficulty discarding. Support for this aspect of the cognitive-behavioral model comes from studies of hoarding beliefs (e.g., the Saving Cognitions Inventory in Chapter 5) and from experimental studies of acquiring and saving (see Chapter 3).

Positive and negative emotional reactions

The personal, family, and cognitive vulnerabilities and mistaken beliefs described above are hypothesized to promote a negative mood (both depression and anxiety) as well as strong positive and negative emotional reactions depending on the context in which objects are being considered. The next section provides more clarification of how these emotions affect behavior.

Avoidance behaviors and hoarding symptoms

Compulsive acquisition and saving are conceptualized as avoidance behaviors designed to stave off feelings of anxiety and grief/loss provoked by thoughts and beliefs about objects. As they increase in frequency, excessive acquiring and saving behaviors eventually lead to an accumulation of clutter that is disorganized due to the lack of information-processing skills (for example, attention, categorization, sorting) as well as faulty beliefs ("I'll make a mistake," "I won't be able to find it again"). Acquiring and saving are reinforced in two ways. They engender strong positive emotions such as pleasure, joy, and excitement, and in addition they prevent or reduce negative feelings like anxiety, guilt, regret, and sadness. For example, a woman who fears that she might waste a useful object avoids feeling guilty by keeping the item she is considering discarding. Similarly, she might purchase an item so she won't regret not having it. This combination of both positive and negative reinforcement creates a compelling motivation to engage in dysfunctional hoarding behaviors, even at the cost of financial and housing stability. This aspect of hoarding also seems to parallel models for understanding addictions. The value of this model of hoarding is evident in the efficacy of the cognitive and behavioral treatment strategies that it has spawned.

Secondary consequences and the vicious cycle

As the hoarding behaviors of excessive acquiring and saving worsen, they lead to disorganized clutter that overwhelms the person's ability to manage their everyday life at home. Impairment in many, if not all, areas of functioning gradually worsens, leading to emotional distress that makes the problem more entrenched through a vicious cycle of misery and compensatory behaviors.

How does this model guide treatment?

Protocols for treating hoarding based on this cognitive-behavioral model contain a range of components intended to address the features described above. They include education about hoarding and beliefs that maintain it; efforts to enhance motivation; cognitive strategies to modify hoarding-related beliefs; skills to improve attention, sorting, organizing, planning, and decision making; and extensive practice in sorting, discarding, and not acquiring possessions. It is not yet clear how genetic factors influence the emergence of hoarding and whether treatments derived from cognitive, behavioral, and developmental models will be useful when there is a strong genetic loading for hoarding. A better understanding of factors such as early attachment problems and the primal need to save objects in order to protect resources and the home environment may enable us to improve treatments and facilitate better outcomes. Certainly, there is plenty of room for additional studies of clinical, neurobiological, and genetic information to expand on the emerging picture of hoarding. Nonetheless, there is already ample support for the cognitive-behavioral model of hoarding described above, as well as its utility in forming the theoretical basis for effective interventions.

Focus on: conceptual models for hoarding

This chapter outlines several compelling models that attempt to explain why hoarding occurs. Among the factors that appear to influence the development of hoarding are genetic predisposition, negative and traumatic life experiences, and depression, but these alone do not explain the many features of HD. Animal models by Dr. Preston are particularly interesting as they clarify that scatter hoarding and larder hoarding are common among animals and these behaviors also occur among humans. It is certainly possible that some hoarding behavior, perhaps even much of it, derives from basic instincts to protect food and dwelling sites. The secure site model proposed by Dr. Kellett incorporates animal models and includes additional human psychological features of anxiety and early attachment. This model suggests that people who hoard are unable to regulate their basic anxiety about security. A model proposed by Dr. Kyrios and colleagues focuses on early attachments to caretakers and self-ambivalence concerns to explain why people are attached to objects that offer security and identity. Finally, a cognitive-behavioral model proposed by Dr. Frost and colleagues has multiple elements that include genetic, familial, and personal vulnerability factors, as well as information-processing problems, that combine to influence beliefs about and meanings of possessions. These in turn provoke positive and/or negative feelings that the person seeks to enjoy (positive) or avoid (negative), leading to excessive acquiring, saving, and disorganized clutter. The aftermath of those symptoms is evident in impairment and distress. Some treatment suggestions derive from these models and are detailed in the coming chapters.

7

WHAT TREATMENTS WORK BEST FOR HOARDING AND ACQUIRING?

The effects of medications and psychotherapy treatments have been studied in clinical settings for people with serious hoarding problems. This chapter describes the treatments that have been investigated and summarizes the findings from those studies with regard to the potential benefits for resolving hoarding symptoms. Given that hoarding disorder (HD) was defined only recently, it is not surprising that research on effective treatments is still quite limited. In general, however, there is good reason to be optimistic that current treatments improve hoarding symptoms, although as yet there is no "gold standard" method.

Do medications work for hoarding?

In fact, very little research has been done on which medications might be effective for treating excessive acquiring and saving problems. The first research studies examined the benefits of medications when hoarding behavior was considered a subtype of obsessive-compulsive disorder (OCD). These studies were focused mainly on a class of drugs known as serotonergic reuptake inhibitors (SRIs). Only a few medication studies have specifically targeted hoarding symptoms, once hoarding was recognized as different from OCD and other OC spectrum conditions. So far, those studies have examined selective serotonergic reuptake inhibitors (SSRIs). The effects of these medications are described below.

SRIs used for OCD

Many studies over the past several decades have demonstrated that medications that target the serotonin system (SRIs and SSRIs) can be very effective for treating OCD symptoms. These medications include such generic drugs such as clomipramine, fluvoxamine, fluoxetine, venlafaxine, and others. Researchers also investigated whether patients with different forms of OCD symptoms might respond differently. For example, did people with contamination and washing problems respond as well as those with harming and checking symptoms? When researchers assessed how well people with hoarding had responded to the medications, the results were mixed: that is, hoarding symptoms did not seem to improve as much as washing, checking, and other OCD symptoms following the use of serotonergic medications. A meta-analysis was conducted to examine the findings from multiple studies that used similar measures of outcome. This analysis showed that patients who had more severe hoarding symptoms had a poorer response to medications that usually worked reasonably well for people with other types of OCD symptoms. In addition, greater severity on hoarding subscales also predicted poorer response in double-blind placebo-controlled studies of citalopram and escitalopram for OCD patients. However, these findings were not confirmed in some other studies where hoarding symptoms did not predict worse outcomes compared to other types of OCD symptoms. This was also true for medication studies of hoarding in children: some medications showed a poor response for children with hoarding symptoms whereas others did not.

These early medication studies were mainly retrospective—that is, the effect on hoarding symptoms was examined after the research had already been concluded and people with hoarding problems were not recruited directly for this research that aimed to test how well medications performed for OCD. This means that the research samples did not contain many people who had serious hoarding problems, and the methods used to identify hoarding symptoms were crude and did not indicate whether the person actually had HD. This makes it difficult to draw any firm conclusions from this research.

More recently, a few prospective studies by Dr. Sanjaya Saxena at UCLA have deliberately recruited people with clinical hoarding symptoms and used better measures of HD diagnosis and outcomes. These studies are described briefly below.

Paroxetine

In 2007 Dr. Saxena and his colleagues reported findings from an open trial of the SRI paroxetine. They compared the outcomes of people who were deliberately recruited for hoarding or for OCD. After 12 weeks of taking the medication, people with hoarding responded as well as those with OCD according to measures of OCD mood and functioning. About 50% of participants with hoarding showed a full or partial response compared to 47% of those with OCD, and hoarding symptoms improved as much as various types of OCD symptoms. Hoarding symptom response was similar to SRI effects on OCD in other studies. Unfortunately, no placebo-controlled studies of paroxetine for HD have been done so far.

Venlafaxine

Dr. Saxena's group also studied the effects of 12 weeks of extended-release venlafaxine for HD in an open-label trial, again without a placebo control. The outcome measures for this study were more detailed and specific to HD. All but 1 of their 24 patients with hoarding finished the trial, an improvement over the 22% dropout rate in the paroxetine study described in the previous paragraph. Among those who completed the medication regimen, 70% were considered "responders," and overall the patients showed a 32% decrease in self-reported Saving Inventory-Revised (SI-R) scores. This suggests that venlafaxine may be helpful for people with HD.

Other medications

Unfortunately, there are no other medication studies—with SRIs or other types of drugs—for HD. A few case reports have reported successful outcomes using various drugs alone and in combination, but this information is not a very helpful guide for medication treatment. Dr. Saxena suggests that clinicians and patients with HD should carefully consider the patients' preferences, co-occurring health and mental health concerns (for example, depression, anxiety disorders, chronic health problems), and potential side effects before deciding whether to try various medications, and dosage adjustments may be needed. It is also possible that medications that improve attention may be helpful for people with attention problems.

Overall, it is not yet possible to recommend specific first-line medication treatments because controlled trials with adequate samples are not available. Among the challenges for testing medication effects is that scientists are not certain what individual medications or combination of medications will best target the array of symptoms that make up HD, including acquiring, executive functioning problems (attention, sorting, organizing, planning, and problem solving), excessive saving (attachment, anxiety), and clutter. Whether the addition of medications to cognitive-behavioral therapy (CBT; described next) might be helpful is also not clear, given that no studies have investigated this combination. Dr. Saxena has reported reasonably good success in combining medications and 6 weeks of intensive treatment focused on discarding, preventing acquiring, organizing, and encouraging alternative behaviors. This combination worked well for 20 people with hoarding problems; the 45% who were considered "responders" had an average of 35% improvement in their self-reported SI-R scores.

How helpful is CBT?

Exposure and response prevention for OCD

Early efforts to treat hoarding followed a standard behavioral therapy protocol for OCD that combined deliberate exposure to feared situations with blocking of ritualistic and avoidant behaviors. However, when this exposure and response prevention (ERP) treatment was applied to people with hoarding problems, it did not work as well according to several studies. A 2014 meta-analysis examined the findings from 21 studies that included more than 300 people with hoarding symptoms. The researchers reported that people with hoarding plus OCD symptoms had a significantly poorer response to traditional OCD treatments compared to those who had OCD without hoarding. They suggested that people who hoard and have other forms of OCD may benefit more from treatments that specifically target their hoarding problems.

Components of CBT for hoarding

As the negative outcomes from ERP studies accumulated in the research literature, it is not surprising that clinical researchers began to develop a separate form of therapy that contained multiple components aimed at specific hoarding symptoms based on the cognitive-behavioral framework for understanding HD described in Chapter 6. Drs. Randy Frost and Gail Steketee were the first to develop and test a type of CBT specifically for hoarding. This treatment includes education about hoarding and acquiring, goal setting and techniques to enhance motivation for treatment, skills training for organizing and decision making, practice resisting urges to acquire, practice sorting and discarding objects, and cognitive therapy aimed at correcting problematic beliefs about possessions. Regular home visits using these methods were part of the program. Although this therapy was initially designed for individual clients, CBT for hoarding has since been effectively adapted for use with groups, as well as self-help, internet, community, and family formats.

Table 7.1 summarizes the core components of CBT for hoarding. Treatment begins with a careful assessment of the hoarding symptoms, associated impairment in functioning, and safety concerns. Comorbid mental health and health problems are also discussed. This information helps the clinician develop a full picture of the client's symptoms and reasons for their hoarding behaviors, known as a case formulation. This case formulation helps the clinician identify appropriate treatment goals, decide on priorities, and select the appropriate treatment components. Clinicians educate clients about the CBT model for understanding hoarding behaviors, and they clarify the rules they will follow during the therapy. For example, clinicians do not touch a client's possessions without permission. Hoarding clients are asked to articulate their personal values and to identify their therapy goals and their overall life goals. They might be encouraged to ask themselves questions like, "Will buying this help me make my home more like I want it?" or "Will getting rid of this make it easier for my children to play at home with their friends?"

Skills training focuses on practicing problem solving, sorting, organizing, and making decisions about whether to acquire, keep, or remove items. Specific behavioral techniques include direct practice in sorting saved objects, discarding those not needed, and not acquiring purchased or free items during outings. Clinicians can help clients use cognitive therapy methods during non-acquiring and discarding practice to change the acquiring and saving beliefs that don't make rational sense to them. For example, the thought "I might need this someday" or "If I don't get this, I might miss an important opportunity" might be replaced with "If I really need it, I'll be able to get it later" or "Not getting this moves me closer to a house I want to live in. There will be other opportunities, and this just seems appealing to me because I'm looking at it right now."

Table 7.1. Clinical Components of CBT for Hoarding

Treatment Components	Strategies
Assessment	Inquire about hoarding symptoms.
	Examine functional impairment and safety concerns.
	Assess related features.
	Assess concurrent health and mental health problems.
Education and Case Formulation	Define and diagnose hoarding.
	Determine treatment goals with the client.
	Clarify the treatment rules (e.g., not touching or removing items without permission).
	Introduce the CBT model and help clients understand how their hoarding developed and why it persists.
Motivation Enhancement	Use motivational interviewing methods.
	Ask client to visualize and describe the desired home.
	Evaluate the costs/benefits of hoarding.
	Identify personal values and long-term life goals.
Skills Training	Categorize, sort, and organize
	Decision making
	Problem solving
Behavioral Experiments and Practice Exposures	Imagine and practice not acquiring additional items.
	Establish categories for keeping and removing items.
	Sort items and decide whether to keep or remove them.
	Experiment with new non-acquiring and discarding behaviors.
	Identify and practice alternative sources of enjoyment.
	Practice ways to cope with discomfort.
	Evaluate the need for others' assistance in clearing spaces.

(continued)

Table 7.1. Continued

Treatment Components	Strategies
Cognitive Techniques	Evaluate beliefs about acquiring and saving possessions.
	Use cognitive strategies during practice sessions for non-acquiring and discarding.
Relapse Prevention	Review new skills learned.
	Identify strategies to maintain new skills.
	Schedule regular personal non-acquiring and discarding sessions.
	Plan booster sessions with clinician.

Therapists also help clients find alternative sources of enjoyment such as going to a social event instead of shopping at a thrift store. They also help clients consider ways to cope with discomfort when they decide not to acquire a new item or when they let go of items, actions that provoke anxiety, guilt, or sadness. Clinicians also use motivational enhancement methods throughout treatment to maintain momentum. Home visits are planned regularly. These visits might be arranged with other people who can be trained to assist (for example, a family friend, a church member, a high school student who can help move boxes). Once good progress has been made, treatment concludes with one or more sessions aimed to prevent relapse.

Individual CBT with a mental health clinician

In 2000, Drs. Steketee and Frost tested the effects of an early version of the methods described above with seven clients who had serious hoarding problems; six of them participated in a CBT group and one in individual therapy. Modest therapy benefits were evident after 15 sessions of CBT over a 20-week period. Acquisition problems improved most, along with changes in beliefs about possessions and improved decision-making and organizational skills. Clutter was slower to change, a finding that persists in recent studies as well. This makes sense since clutter is the consequence of excessive acquisition, saving, and disorganization. Three clients who continued individual treatment twice a month for a year reported more gains in all areas.

In the next phase of treatment development, Drs. Tolin, Frost, and Steketee tested a revised version of CBT containing all of the elements listed in Table 7.1, including monthly home visits to practice skills. Trained therapists followed a treatment manual and clients used a workbook to help them practice the procedures. An initial pilot study of 14 people who met criteria for HD showed that 26 sessions of treatment over 7 to 12 months led to significant improvement in 5 of the 10 people who completed the treatment, but unfortunately 4 people did not finish the trial.

Subsequently, these researchers completed a waitlist-controlled study of 46 people with HD who were randomly assigned to CBT or to a 12-week waitlist before starting the trial. Those who received the CBT intervention had significantly better outcomes on hoarding severity after 12 weeks than people on the waitlist. For those who completed all 26 sessions of CBT, therapists considered 71% to be "much" or "very much" improved and 81% of the clients rated themselves in this category. However, only 41% of the group met criteria for "clinically significantly improvement" indicating that behavior was similar to that of people without a hoarding problem. Most people were able to maintain their gains up to 1 year later, when 62% had therapist ratings of "much" or "very much" improved and 79% had self-ratings in this category. The few men who participated did not benefit as much as women. More severe initial hoarding symptoms, perfectionism, and social anxiety were associated with worse outcomes. Perfectionism was an especially problematic predictor of outcomes at 1-year follow-up. Some patients refused the CBT and a few failed to follow instructions, provoking questions about how best to provide CBT treatment.

Group CBT

A variety of delivery formats for the CBT strategies for hoarding described above have also been studied. These include therapist-guided groups, peer-led groups, and web-based groups, mainly tested in open trials and waitlist-controlled trials. A few studies have compared treatments.

The individual CBT manual that was modified for delivery with groups has produced promising results. In most studies, groups have included 6 to 12 people who received 15 to 20 sessions of group therapy for 90 minutes to 2 hours. The group treatment approaches differed a little across the studies: some included home visits and/or non-professional assistants whereas others did not. Overall, a meta-analysis showed that the outcomes from several clinician-led group treatments were only slightly and not significantly lower than those achieved by individual therapy. Two group treatment manuals have been published, both with companion client workbooks that clients use to complete the exercises: Muroff, Underwood, and Steketee's *Group Treatment for Hoarding Disorder* and Tolin and colleagues' *CBT for Hoarding Disorder: A Group Therapy Program*.

Peer-led groups have also been studied as a method for delivering hoarding treatment. These are short-term (usually 12–15 sessions), action-oriented groups that go beyond traditional self-help groups by using the book *Buried in Treasures* to guide the group's work. This book was deliberately designed to mirror the CBT hoarding treatment manual by Drs. Steketee and Frost and is aimed at helping clients practice new skills and actions that promote improvements in hoarding symptoms. Known as "BIT Workshops," these peer-led groups have led to significant decreases in hoarding symptoms (about 24%) that approach the benefits from individual CBT and therapist-led CBT groups for hoarding. Not surprisingly, a number of BIT Workshop participants continue to experience hoarding symptoms after completing these relatively brief groups. In particular, clutter tends to change more slowly than other hoarding behaviors. Some support groups have repeated the BIT Workshop experience in order to bolster their skills to reduce hoarding symptoms. The peer-led groups may be especially helpful for people who are reluctant to admit the extent of their hoarding problem: they would avoid working with a mental health therapist but would feel more comfortable working alongside others who share their problem.

Finally, technology has been used to help people who hoard through both web-based and video-enhanced online CBT. These internet and video-assisted methods have been studied mainly in open trials with individuals or online groups. Individual web-based CBT has been successfully used by clinicians who "visit" clients in their homes through laptop or tablet web-based live video programs. The clients learn and practice CBT methods at the therapist's direction, and progress on clutter is evident from the pictures transmitted through the internet. In this way, people with hoarding problems can receive "home visits" on a regular basis to work through skills training and practice discarding and even non-acquiring. One study found good results using a blend of 12 weeks of face-to-face group CBT plus an 8-week therapist-assisted CBT program accessed through the web. A pilot study showed that the significant improvement achieved by these online interventions continued to improve after the initial group intervention. It seems likely that future treatments for HD will be facilitated by or even fully conducted through the internet.

Comparisons of group and individual treatments

Findings from the various studies of CBT outcomes for HD were examined in a 2014 meta-analysis to understand the overall trends in the research findings. At that time, 10 studies of CBT had reported findings for 12 different groups that included a total of 232 people treated for HD. The length of treatment ranged from 13 sessions for peer-led groups to 26 to 35 sessions for individual treatment, a considerable range of time. All of the individual therapy studies included periodic in-home sessions, and home visits were also used in three of the five therapist-led group treatments. The analysis indicated that all of the interventions produced statistically significant improvement in hoarding symptoms compared to baseline scores. The treatment effects for both individual and group CBT were considered to be large, suggesting that most patients benefited.

Difficulty discarding was a target symptom for all of the CBT interventions and seemed to improve most. In addition, clutter was reduced and general functioning improved to some extent. It is not surprising that clutter and functioning improved more modestly given that clutter is a byproduct of difficulty discarding and excessive acquiring and often takes more time to resolve, especially in severe cases. When the investigators examined factors that might predict who benefited most and least across these studies, they found that men fared worse, as did those who were older, received fewer sessions, and had fewer home visits. Most patients showed consistent improvement in hoarding severity, although the number of people with "clinically significant change" ranged from only 24% to 43%. In practice, this means that most participants still had post-treatment hoarding scores in the clinical range.

What about treatments for special populations?

So far, we have discussed mainly CBT methods applied to middle-aged adults who are seeking treatment for HD. But what about children, older adults, and those who hoard animals? Also, might other methods of therapy be useful? This section reviews the limited research on these issues.

Treating older adults with hoarding

Both individual and group CBT methods have also been tested for older adults. The results suggested a need for some modifications. As described in Chapters 1 and 2, impairment in functioning combined with age-related cognitive decline makes hoarding in older adults an especially challenging problem. Unfortunately, there is little evidence that hoarding symptoms decrease over the life course. Because of the typically chronic and worsening course of hoarding, people whose hoarding symptoms begin early in life can have very serious problems as they age. The adverse consequences of hoarding in the elderly can include lack of regular medical care, difficulty managing medications, problems with diet and nutrition, and worsening medical conditions, especially pulmonary and cardiac problems. Older adults with hoarding are also prone to ambulatory problems and falls. They can become socially isolated, hiding their hoarding behavior until a medical or housing problem leads to the arrival of first responders who arrive to find unlivable home conditions. Clinical treatment can help mitigate the shame and embarrassment and forestall housing relocation. The assessment of hoarding in older adults is similar to that described in Chapter 5 unless there is marked cognitive decline that would make a person's responses invalid. A comprehensive assessment should include a clinical interview, home visits, reports from family or friends (if possible), a neurocognitive assessment, determination of functioning, and evaluation of other health and mental health problems.

When Dr. Catherine Ayers and her colleagues tested standard CBT for hoarding in older adults in an open trial, unfortunately they found less benefit than other researchers had observed for middle-aged adults. To address the problems they observed, they modified the standard treatment by adding cognitive rehabilitation methods and focusing the behavioral techniques mainly on skills training and direct practice, with limited use of cognitive therapy methods that older adults found difficult to understand and apply. Exposure activities were modified to fit the patient's mobility and energy level. They labeled this treatment CREST, which stands for cognitive rehabilitation (teaching skills to improve memory, planning, cognitive flexibility, and problem solving) and exposure/ sorting therapy. They conducted a randomized controlled trial that compared CREST to geriatric case management (CM) for 58 older adults with HD. Both treatments contained 26 individual sessions over a 6-month period with several home visits from CREST therapists or CM nurses. The CREST participants improved significantly more—52% were considered treatment responders compared to only 16% for CM. The CREST benefits were also maintained at a 6-month follow-up. More information on these outcomes is given in Chapter 10.

Accordingly, treatment for older adults should focus especially on cognitive skills training and sorting and non-acquiring practice that aims to clear clutter and reduce the potential for harm. Older adults with some cognitive impairment can use aspects of the treatment, and the focus on harm reduction is an important element for enhancing motivation, especially in the face of treatment refusal. The older adult should be included as part of a harm-reduction team member alongside family, friends, clinicians, and other human services professionals whose goals are to reduce the risks in the home.

Treating children with hoarding

Although hoarding behavior begins on average during the teenage years and is known to affect younger children (see Chapter 1), very little research on treatment is available for this age group. The existing case studies of hoarding treatment in children come mainly from those who seek help in OCD clinics. Dr. Eric Storch and his colleagues have used a type of CBT for children that involves the parents or other caregivers. The CBT modules include practice discarding and not acquiring, prevention of hoarding behaviors, basic cognitive strategies to evaluate beliefs about possessions, and training parents in behavioral management using reinforcement strategies. This treatment has been effective in case studies, but unfortunately no large-scale trials have been done so far. Similarly, only a few case studies have examined pharmacotherapy for hoarding in children.

Treating people who hoard animals

Although animal hoarding can be a very serious problem, as noted in Chapter 1, relatively little research has been done on this problem, and even less on treatments. Many studies of animal hoarding report that 60% to 100% of people who have animals legally removed from their care acquire more animals, indicating that simply removing animals is unlikely to improve most animal-hoarding behavior. Although no studies of treatment outcomes have been published, occasional case examples describe people who have stopped hoarding animals, but these cases seem to be exceptions rather than the rule. Although courts sometimes mandate counseling, no proven therapy for animal hoarding is available, so it is not clear how to refer people to appropriate clinicians. In addition, many people who have been adjudicated for animal hoarding are reluctant to participate in therapy, making it difficult to enforce mandated psychotherapy referrals. The most appropriate method for engaging people with animal hoarding is likely to be through multidisciplinary community hoarding task forces (see Chapter 9), where task force members can work together to help people who hoard animals identify useful personal goals that meet court-mandated compliance requirements. Limiting the number of animals will be a necessary goal in cases of animal neglect for overwhelmed caregivers and rescuers, whereas abstinence is likely to be essential in cases of overt animal cruelty by those who exploit animals.

Intervention should include efforts to provide basic social supports that meet clients' needs for social bonds that were previously provided by animals. Given the longstanding nature of the problems that seem to contribute to animal hoarding, even with a cooperative and receptive person, it is likely that effective intervention will require significant treatment time and periodic checks on compliance with court mandates.

Other therapy methods

CBT designed specifically for HD is the best-tested method of treatment. However, the alternative and/or complementary models of hoarding described in Chapter 6 imply that additional intervention methods may be useful. For example, when strong attachment to objects is accompanied by an early history of missing, neglectful, or abusive parents or caretakers, a focus on self-identity and relationships with others may be important to reduce feelings of uncertainty and threat. An interesting open trial study by Dr. Kieron O'Connor examined outcomes for hoarding of a treatment called inference-based therapy. In this method, the therapist helps clients understand how their imaginary narratives about objects (for example, "I might need this someday," "Think of the possibilities," "Keeping this prevents waste") influence their emotions and behaviors. The therapy also connects their hoarding beliefs and behaviors to doubts about themselves and connects this to insecure early attachments and anxieties about objects. Reasonably good results were evident after 20 weeks of therapy and at a 6-month follow-up, with 28% achieving improvement that made a significant difference in their lives.

Because at least some people who hoard are especially sensitive to feelings of anxiety and have difficulty regulating their emotions (see Chapter 3), the addition of techniques from a therapeutic approach known as dialectical behavior therapy, such as mindfulness and emotion regulation, may be useful. Strategies to help with emotion regulation are likely to be especially useful for people with additional psychiatric problems that generate considerable distress (for example, depression, bipolar disorder, and impulse-control problems like compulsive buying). However, so far, these methods have not yet been tested for people with HD. Motivational interviewing strategies are essential accompaniments to CBT for those with limited insight who are not actively seeking treatment. In fact, motivational enhancements are often needed even for motivated clients who will inevitably struggle to part with possessions as they practice discarding.

Focus on: treatment for hoarding

Multiple studies indicate that CBT that specifically targets hoarding symptoms is effective and can be delivered in a wide variety of formats—individual and group therapy, peerled groups, and web-based individual and group treatment. However, there is considerable room for improvement in the outcomes of these CBT methods. Foremost among the concerns is that across all of the treatment research on CBT for hoarding, the rates of clinically significant change tend to be modest, leaving many participants still meeting criteria for an HD diagnosis. In addition, most of the patients studied have been white women, so we do not know how well these treatments work for people from diverse backgrounds. More research on larger and broader samples is needed.

It appears that older adults respond best to a modified CBT method that focuses more on cognitive rehabilitation strategies and direct practice efforts than on changing beliefs through cognitive therapy methods. Although few studies have been done with children who hoard, including parents and guardians in treatment is essential. Other therapy methods that help clients manage their emotional sensitivity may enhance CBT outcomes. However, more research is needed to guide therapy choices, as well as more skilled clinicians and other professionals or peers who can lead treatment efforts.

8

HOW CAN FAMILY MEMBERS AND OTHER METHODS HELP WITH HOARDING?

In addition to the treatment methods described in Chapter 7, a few other methods may be helpful for family members and for those who suffer from hoarding symptoms. In considering alternative ways to resolve hoarding problems, it is important to distinguish clutter from hoarding disorder (HD), especially as the media do not always make this distinction clear. Remember that clutter alone does not define HD; to meet HD criteria, the person must have specific problems parting with objects, and that's why the clutter accumulates. The person also experiences distress at discarding and their symptoms cause significant impairment in functioning and the use of the home. It is likely that when difficulty discarding and clutter occur in a mild form that would not qualify for an HD diagnosis, self-help efforts and support groups will be helpful. But given that hoarding behavior usually worsens with time, serious symptoms are likely to require specialized help from professionals who are experienced in treating this problem.

The treatments described previously and the methods discussed in this chapter constitute a potential "stepped care" model for intervention in which hoarding is treated with the least cost and effort required to match the severity of the symptoms and the person's preferences. For example, someone with mild acquiring and saving might benefit just by reading *Buried in Treasures* or another self-help book, whereas a person with moderate symptoms who enjoys socializing may respond well to a peer-led group using the same book. Those with more serious symptoms might require help from a clinician in the form of individual therapy or group treatment described in Chapter 7. Family members who educate themselves about hoarding can undoubtedly be helpful no matter what level of severity is present. Consider the family and other intervention methods described below in light of a stepped-care approach that aims to match the intervention to the person's needs.

How do you know when a family member has hoarding problems?

Approximately 80% of people with hoarding problems live with family members or have some contact with family and friends. Spouses, partners, children, and others—especially those who live in the home—have daily experiences with the family member's collecting, saving, and difficulty discarding. This can lead to strong feelings that range from compassion to condemnation. Of course, these feelings influence their degree of involvement with the person who is hoarding and their willingness to assist them. The complicated nature of hoarding, including information-processing problems, beliefs about objects, and strong emotions (see Chapter 6), can sometimes make it difficult to know whether there is an actual problem with hoarding. Drs. Michael Tompkins and Tamara Hartl offer family members a helpful checklist of warning signs that signal a problem:

- The home or parts of it are off limits to others
- Regular acquiring of too many things
- Difficulty letting go of or discarding objects
- Difficulty making decisions, organizing, sorting, or categorizing
- Compromised safety or reduced comfort when using the spaces in the home
- Increased discussion about the state of the home, acquiring, or saving.

Although these features might signal a hoarding problem, it is important to remember that there is considerable variability (even within families) in how people decide what is worth saving, how much is enough, how items are organized, and how spaces and objects are used in the home. These differences can spark disagreement between family members and the person who is hoarding. A family member who suspects that hoarding is the problem should consider the root of the behavior in guiding the next help-seeking steps. As discussed in Chapter 1, hoarding may be the primary problem, or acquiring and difficulty discarding may be the result of another mental or physical health problem such as major depression, obsessive-compulsive disorder, dementia, brain injury, and mobility problems.

How can family members help?

Family members' reactions, whether frustration or concern or a combination of both, are likely to influence their efforts to help and the outcome. Sometimes spouses, partners, and children who are angry and resentful undertake to clear the clutter without the knowledge or permission of the person who is doing the hoarding. Clearing rooms, removing or relocating items, or repeated and forceful use of persuasion or bargaining usually engenders anger, hostility, defiance, and disengagement in the person who is hoarding. Though the clearing and cleaning efforts may be well intentioned, they are often experienced as intrusive and subversive acts. Even gentler tactics like subtly pointing out the problem or commenting on the impact of the stuff on the person and their quality of life may be met with resistance and denial. Although walking away from the family member who is hoarding may seem attractive, worry about health and safety consequences and a basic sense of family commitment often translate into a desire to stay close and try something different. Toward that end, we highly recommend Drs. Michael Tompkins and Tamara Hartl's harm-reduction approach to hoarding intervention. They describe this in detail in their book *Digging Out: Helping Your Loved One Manage Clutter, Hoarding, and Compulsive Acquiring*. We will borrow heavily from their writings here and encourage family readers to use their book as a guide.

Harm reduction

Harm reduction is a set of principles developed within the public health field aimed at reducing the potential negative consequences of a behavior (like hoarding) through incremental behavioral changes. The aim of a harm-reduction approach for hoarding is to minimize the potential for harm to self and others through changes in acquiring and saving behavior. The initial goal is not to eliminate the behaviors but to reduce their intensity. Taking the perspective that it is possible for someone to live in a healthy and safe way even if they continue to engage in some hoarding behavior can be challenging, at least initially. This is especially true if the hoarding behavior is viewed through a moral lens as a "bad behavior" that needs to stop. However, if family members can agree that reducing the risk of harm due to hoarding is a worthy goal, this approach is especially helpful.

Drs. Tompkins and Hartl recommend that family members undertake harm reduction for hoarding with a spirit of acceptance of their loved one's viewpoints as valid while insisting on safety. They suggest that adopting such a spirit is perhaps even more valuable than the harm-reduction plan itself. Some of the guiding principles in harm reduction are (1) do no harm, (2) it's not necessary to stop all hoarding behaviors, (3) each situation is different, and (4) change is slow. They further encourage family members to remember that no two hoarding situations are identical, their loved one is an essential member of the harm-reduction team, and their loved one may have other more pressing problems to address.

Making a harm-reduction plan

As outlined by Drs. Tompkins and Hartl, a harm-reduction plan for hoarding comprises five main elements:

1. Engage the person who hoards in the harm-reduction approach.
2. Build the harm-reduction team.
3. Assess the potential for harm.
4. Create the harm- reduction plan.
5. Implement the plan.

Ideally, family members would systematically proceed through each step of the process. Although harm reduction de-emphasizes discarding and may be more appealing than clinical treatment described in Chapter 7, engaging family members who hoard can still be challenging, especially if they have limited insight and/or a history past of negative experiences from outside regulatory agencies about the clutter that caused mistrust. Negative past experiences naturally lead to reluctance to accept any offers of help.

Motivational interviewing (MI) strategies aimed at raising and resolving ambivalence about making changes to hoarding behavior are particularly helpful in the initial engagement phase (see Miller & Rollnick, 2012, for more information on MI). Developing skills to enhance motivation requires training and lots of practice for effective use, but family members can learn some basic strategies to facilitate family conversations without professional help. Unfortunately, approaching conversations about hoarding without some motivational skills can aggravate an already difficult situation and increase the conflict and distance between family members around hoarding. If this happens, families may wish to engage an MI-trained clinician to guide their family conversations about hoarding. A trained professional can help family members gain important insights from the person who is hoarding. It allows all perspectives to be heard and valued, thereby better preserving the family relationships.

In addition to the person who is hoarding, family members are primary players in advancing harm reduction for the entire hoarding team. Friends, members of the faith community, neighbors, and human services professionals (protective service workers, housing providers, and public health officials and nurses) are stakeholders who are also members of the harm-reduction team. Clarifying everyone's role, expectations, outcomes, and timelines is an important way to ensure a collaborative harm-reduction approach that facilitates the best possible outcomes.

After assembling the harm-reduction team, families can assist by getting a clear picture of the hoarding situation. This means intentionally assessing (1) the environment, (2) the person's needs, and (3) the available supports. The environmental assessment includes a careful examination of the home, including the volume of clutter, whether squalid conditions are present, and risks like tripping hazards, fire hazards, and insect or animal infestations. An objective assessment is best accomplished by talking with the person who hoards in order to understand how motivated they are to change, factors that might facilitate progress (for example, financial resources), and barriers like physical health problems that interfere with working on the hoarding behavior. Finally, assessment of available supports requires considering the person's natural support systems such as family members, networks of friends and acquaintances, and organizations that can help support the harm-reduction plan.

Once the assessment is completed, family members can help develop the harm-reduction plan by working collaboratively with their loved one who hoards. Drs. Tompkins and Hartl recommend that the plan be formalized in writing to include the specific harm-reduction targets, how often work will occur in the home, what resources or supplies are needed, and the role of each team member. Appropriate targets include not only clearing clutter from high-risk areas (for example, removing papers from around the stove and oven) but also implementing systems to maintain gains and prevent back-sliding (for example, putting a basket near the sofa to store papers away from the stove). The harm-reduction plan may also involve securing and maintaining support systems to prevent the reaccumulation of clutter.

After the team is assembled and the plan is developed, the process begins. The team's efforts continue as long as necessary to reduce or eliminate the risks caused by the acquiring and saving. It's useful to remember that part of the harm-reduction plan should be to support the person who is hoarding and facilitate their continued engagement. The primary focus is always on safety; comfort and attractiveness are secondary.

Should family members get professional help?

Many people who hoard are limited in their ability to recognize the hoarding problem and its impact on others. This is one of the most frustrating aspects of hoarding for family members. Strained relationships and great burden may result. Sadly, sometimes partners or spouses find it impossible to continue their relationship because of the amassed clutter and the relationship tension and decide to pursue a temporary separation or even divorce. Siblings, adult children, and others often feel significant distress, embarrassment, and shame that leads to additional mental or physical health problems and to a rupture in the relationship with the loved one who is hoarding. When dependent children or older adults who live in a hoarded environment experience difficulty achieving developmental milestones or carrying out daily activities, this indicates unsafe living conditions for these specially protected groups. Adult children who grew up in hoarded homes and repeatedly experienced the unwanted consequences of the hoarding are likely to feel hostility that interferes with their ability to develop a compassionate response to their parent's situation. When these circumstances are present, family members are likely to benefit from seeking professional help to manage the hoarding situation.

Thoughts such as "I should be able to help my family member," "If I can't help them there's something wrong with me," and "I'm so embarrassed, I can't tell anyone what's going on" can lead family members to suffer silently in an uncomfortable and unsafe situation. Feelings of regret, shame, and fear are also obstacles to seeking help. Sometimes, however, the most useful next step a family member can take is to recognize the limits of their capacity and know that however sincere their efforts to support their family member's goals for a better life, the most productive and useful course of action may be to seek outside professional help for the hoarding problem.

The practical problems associated with hoarding and interpersonal difficulties that interfere in family functioning often necessitate somewhat different help-seeking responses. For instance, in situations where a minor child is adversely affected by the hoarding, a referral to a child welfare organization may be the most prudent response to protect the child and to access community resources needed to reduce hoarding behavior. In cases where a frail older adult is unable to attend to their physical health and basic nutritional needs owing to a too-full house, adult protective services may be the most appropriate referral. Anecdotally, family members often find it very difficult to make referrals of this kind because it feels disloyal to their loved one. However, it is essential that the risk of imminent harm is addressed immediately. Contact with human service organizations can be a gateway to finding helpful resource networks that may be otherwise inaccessible.

Mental health support for the person who is hoarding and for family members willing to participate is often a helpful course of action, especially when family relationships are distressed. As described earlier, clinical support to enhance motivation and increase readiness for change is especially important. Families can also find support to maintain a helpful attitude and to implement the harm-reduction strategies for hoarding intervention as described above. Additional tools can be provided by the therapist, including education about hoarding and other mental health problems that is presented to all participating family members. Psychological education is also a vehicle for correcting mistaken assumptions and clarifying points of confusion, especially in distinguishing personal character flaws from the clinical features of hoarding.

Mental health practitioners can also help people who hoard and their family members to learn effective communication strategies such as using "I" statements and conveying genuine concern when discussing the problematic hoarding. An emerging model of clinical support for families affected by hoarding is the Family as Motivators (FAM) training program that aims to increase treatment-seeking behavior and readiness for change among people who hoard, as well as improve the well-being of family members. FAM training modules include psychoeducation, harm reduction, and MI. In addition, FAM focuses on reducing family accommodation in which family members unwittingly engage in activities that reinforce the primary features of hoarding—acquiring, saving, and difficulty discarding. In a pilot study of this method, the training was delivered in 1- to 2-hour sessions across 14 weeks in a clinical setting. Although the results are still preliminary, positive trends were evident as family members reported good use of coping strategies, increased hopefulness, increased understanding of motivational techniques, reduced family accommodation, and reduced negative impact of hoarding on the family. Further study is needed to confirm these initial findings.

Can I get help from the internet?

The internet is an excellent source of information about hoarding problems. Below are listed various professional association websites with such information:

- International OCD Foundation (IOCDF) maintains an informational website on hoarding (www.iocdf.org/hoarding) with referral listings for therapists, clinics and programs, support groups, and organizations by geographic area and specialization (which includes the option to select hoarding).

- Anxiety and Depression Association of America (www.adaa.org)
- Association for Behavioral and Cognitive Therapies (www.abct.org)
- American Psychiatric Association (www.psychiatry.org/patients-families/hoarding-disorder)
- American Psychological Association through their *Psychology Today* forum (www.psychologytoday.com/us/conditions/hoarding-disorder)

Most of these organizations also provide referral information on the web to guide hoarding sufferers and family members to appropriate treatment in their geographic area. A number of other websites can also be useful, but readers should use caution, especially as social media and popular press sites tend to sensationalize hoarding, and some sites are simply recruitment tools for their services.

In addition, some web-based apps intended for hoarding symptoms may prove helpful. For example, the Clutter Image Rating scale, developed by Dr. Jordana Muroff and colleagues at Boston University, has been adapted to assist people who hoard in keeping track of progress in reducing clutter; it is available online. Another downloadable app to address acquiring problems is from Life-Pod, a professional organizing group in the United Kingdom. This app focuses on goals, strategies, journaling, and tracking progress following a number of the cognitive-behavioral therapy (CBT) methods for HD. Strategies include establishing rules for making decisions about acquiring, "rerouting" to develop alternative activities to replace excessive acquiring, ruminating to evaluate the advantages and disadvantages of acquiring, and rewards to reinforce goal achievement. The journal invites the user to respond to questions about acquiring, including need versus want, and the tracker tool can be used to list acquired and not acquired items as well as costs/savings. No doubt additional web-based apps will appear in the coming years, and hopefully these methods will be studied to determine how helpful they are in reducing acquiring, difficulty discarding, and clutter.

Are there self-help books I can read?

A quick online search produced an impressive list of over 1,000 self-help books aimed at helping people organize their homes and reduce clutter. These decluttering books are often intended for people with moderate clutter and messy homes, but not necessarily for those whose symptoms, impairment, and distress qualify for an HD diagnosis. A few of these self-help books for hoarding have been written by mental health professionals with extensive clinical experience in treating people with HD. They include:

- Drs. David Tolin, Randy O. Frost, and Gail Steketee, *Buried in Treasures: Help for Compulsive Acquiring, Saving and Hoarding,* 2007 (1st edition), 2014 (2nd edition), Oxford University Press
- Dr. Robin Zasio, *The Hoarder in You: How to Live a Happier, Healthier, Uncluttered Life,* 2012, Rodale Press
- Drs. Jerome Bubrick, Fugen Neziroglu, and Jose Yaryura-Tobias, *Overcoming Compulsive Hoarding: Why You Save and How You Can Stop,* 2004, New Harbinger Press.

Among these books, *Buried in Treasures* was designed to closely follow the CBT protocol outlined in Steketee and Frost's therapist guide *Treatment for Hoarding Disorder,* which is based on research on the problem of hoarding and its treatment (see summary of this treatment program in Chapter 7). However, there is limited evidence to indicate that reading a book and trying to follow the instructions improves serious hoarding problems to a significant degree. To our knowledge, the only test of the benefits of such "bibliotherapy" was conducted by Dr. Muroff, who compared the outcomes of those who read *Buried in Treasures* to those who participated in a therapist-guided group treatment for HD over a 20-week period. The bibliotherapy participants achieved a 9% improvement in symptoms compared to average gains of 25% to 30% for those participating in group CBT. This suggests that a few individuals with HD do benefit from reading and following a CBT protocol on their own. Perhaps those with mild to moderate symptoms and/or limited comorbidity may benefit most from this strategy.

As noted in Chapter 7, when *Buried in Treasures* was used by peer support leaders as the organizing structure for 12- to 15-week "BIT Workshops," the participants' hoarding behaviors improved substantially more—about 24%, compared to 9% for Dr. Muroff's bibliotherapy sample. This suggests that when used consistently in a group format, a book that details the methods used effectively in clinical therapy can be a very useful guide in reducing hoarding problems.

Will joining a support group help?

The IOCDF website lists various support groups that may be of interest to people with hoarding problems, but keep in mind that so far there are no studies of the actual benefits of support group participation in reducing hoarding behaviors. This means that people with hoarding problems should not expect a support group to resolve their problem, but it may be especially useful in helping reduce feelings of embarrassment and shame and also as a way to develop more insight and motivation to work on the problem. In addition, both Clutterers Anonymous and Messies Anonymous groups offer 12-step programs for hoarding, although no research has been done to show that a 12-step program is beneficial for reducing hoarding symptoms. In addition, the IOCDF website lists support groups by geographic area and also sponsors several of these during its annual conference in July. Some of the other professional mental health organizations mentioned earlier in this chapter also list support groups on their referral sites. In any case, support groups are an excellent way to seek social and practical support for working to reduce the excessive acquiring, difficulty discarding, and clutter that characterize HD. However, they may not by themselves solve the problem without additional assistance from trained professionals and peers.

Will hiring a professional organizer help?

Many self-help books have also been written by professional organizers who are also members of the National Association of Professional Organizers (www.napo.net) and/or the Institute for Challenging Disorganization (ICD) (www.challengingdisorganization.org). Both of these organizations maintain geographically identified referral listings through their websites. The latter group represents a specialization within professional organizing that addresses aspects of HD. ICD has established a formal training program for assisting people in organizing their homes and businesses. Some professional organizers have obtained specialized training to learn skills to work with hoarding-related problems such as attention deficit, difficulty with decision making, excessive acquiring, and strong attachment to possessions that interferes with discarding. Engaging a professional organizer may carry less stigma for some people with HD than seeking mental health treatment and therefore may be an important opportunity to work on hoarding symptoms.

In her book on professional organizing and hoarding, Judith Kolberg writes that those with hoarding share common ground with people who are chronically disorganized, as attention-deficit disorder and physical challenges can contribute to hoarding behavior. However, important differences include the stronger emotional attachment to possessions of people with HD that extends to a wide range of items, as well as intense feelings of shame about clutter. Those who hoard often have an excessive number of items that others consider useless or of little value, whereas those with chronic disorganization may have many objects that most people view as useful or valuable. However, research on specific distinctions between chronic disorganization and HD is lacking.

Professional organizers often work collaboratively with other professionals (e.g., psychiatrist, psychologist, social worker, family member, home health aide, housing coordinator) to provide services to clients with serious hoarding behaviors. Their role is to help clients learn to sort and develop organizing systems and to provide structure and motivation to complete work at home. Most professional organizers require private payment, although occasionally public funds may pay for services through organizations that serve the disabled and elderly. Professional organizers can be very helpful in treating hoarding, and some aspects of CBT for hoarding (see Chapter 7) are drawn from professional organizing practices. Because professional organizers are not mandated reporters, they may not recognize hoarding situations that violate the rights of vulnerable individuals or fail to meet safety and health codes. At the same time, they have developed specific tools to assess clutter and disorganization, although to our knowledge no formal research has been done on the validity and reliability of these measures or on the impact of professional organizing interventions for hoarding.

Focus on: families and other sources of help for hoarding

Hoarding presents a number of challenging problems, including health and safety risks, that have an adverse impact on the person who is hoarding and their family members. Tensions result from differing opinions about the need to address the problem, and strong emotions often arise in determining the best strategies for tackling the problematic saving and acquiring behavior. Resistance and mistrust commonly characterize interactions between family members and the loved one who is hoarding. Strategies to reduce harm, enhance motivation, and improve communication skills can be helpful to both sufferers and family members in reducing these unwanted negative interactions. Trained mental health clinicians can help families learn communication and motivational skills.

Alternatives to individual and group treatment by mental health professionals and peer-led groups are available, although in most cases no research is available to provide guidance about which methods will work best. Options include seeking information and referrals from professional organizations and related websites and use of hoarding apps designed to track clutter and reduce acquiring. Among the many self-help books on organizing and clutter are a few written by mental health professionals with extensive experience in treating HD. Among these, one has been tested as a standalone treatment with limited success and generally good success when used in a peer-led group context. Support groups may be helpful, especially in reducing stigma and increasing motivation to work on the problem. Professional organizers who are trained to assist with hoarding problems can be helpful, often in conjunction with mental health treatment. These strategies can be applied in a stepped-care model where the intensity of the intervention is matched to the severity and complexity of the hoarding and related symptoms.

9

HOW CAN COMMUNITIES HELP WITH HOARDING?

Isn't my home my castle?

Throughout most of North America, housekeeping practices and the manner in which someone choses to keep their home are considered private matters. This is especially true when the person has rights of ownership to their dwelling. However, there are certain circumstances wherein the community has a legitimate interest in what happens "behind closed doors." In the early chapters of this book we detailed notions of hoarding as a (private) mental health problem. In this chapter, we discuss the extension of our understanding of hoarding as a complex mental health and public/social problem that may necessitate community involvement.

As we've described earlier, problematic hoarding has consequences that include an increase in health and safety risks for the person who is hoarding and for those living in or near the hoarded residence. Accumulated possessions can block window and door exits and generate hazards for falling and being crushed. Large quantities of saved objects like paper, clothing, and books that are highly combustible produce threatening environments where fire is likely to spread more quickly and to burn at higher temperatures compared to non-hoarded homes. Such hoarding situations are a source of potential danger not only for those living within that unit, but also for people in neighboring units and buildings. Furthermore, saving a large volume of stuff often interferes with necessary repairs on plumbing, sewage, electrical, and heating systems that are not functioning adequately to provide a safe and comfortable home. Often, the home dweller delays calling in service personnel due to embarrassment and fear of discovery, and a severely hoarded environment renders access to the affected service area almost impossible.

In addition, the wide array of saved objects and the debilitated state of the home can lead to squalid conditions. Described as filth or degradation from neglect, squalor is commonly characterized by the presence of rotting food, human or animal urine and/or feces, and insect or rodent infestations. Such situations are especially problematic for neighbors who share walls (e.g., apartments, condominiums, townhouses). All of these hazardous conditions may require immediate attention from community first responders and human services providers. Their necessary actions belie the notion that hoarding is a private problem that can be addressed strictly at an individual or familial level.

Thus, severe hoarding can pit personal rights against the public good, generating complicated societal questions. Determining the level of threat by considering the real risk to person and property is a difficult matter, and often there are no easy answers. Some community organizations and service providers are under legal and regulatory mandates to take action to ameliorate conditions in the home that are deemed a public health risk. Likewise, some sectors of human services are required by law to investigate and act when there is undue risk of harm to a protected class of citizens, such as children, disabled individuals, and older adults. In this chapter we explore community-based responses to hoarding that include enforcement of health and housing codes and other laws, as well as supportive interventions.

Who is responsible for health and safety risks due to hoarding?

Community agencies that become involved in hoarding situations are typically responding to very severe and complex cases wherein the person has limited insight about the impact of their behavior and limited motivation to address the problem. These two factors, combined with the social stigmatization of hoarding, mean that people who hoard are often reluctant to acknowledge that they have a problem, and also reluctant to accept direct offers of help or referrals for specific interventions. Human services providers who recognize and understand these challenges are most likely to provide effective services by first building a trusting relationship through a collaborative approach in order to reduce potential risks and achieve compliance with regulatory mandates.

Below are brief descriptions of the human services sectors that commonly become involved when homes are dangerously full of stuff and people are at increased risk of harm. There are regional and national differences in how these types of agencies are organized and in the terminology used to describe the professional roles and tasks. Here, we try to use the most common terms.

Housing

Housing providers are often the first to encounter accumulations of clutter that signal problematic hoarding. These include landlords, property managers, providers of subsidized and/or supportive housing, and contracted housing organizations. These housing settings often provide the initial point of entry for hoarding interventions. Guided by federal and state legislation, housing providers have a responsibility to identify and rectify housing or sanitary code violations that result from hoarding—for example, blocked exits, nonfunctioning utilities, or the presence of squalor. In the case of supported public housing available to people who meet income or need requirements, the funding agency may make its financial support contingent on compliance with housing regulations. This serves as a significant incentive for housing providers and managers to attend to hoarding sooner rather than later. When owners and managers of privately owned rental properties must intervene for homes with potentially hazardous conditions due to hoarding, they must balance the tenant's privacy rights against the homeowner's property rights.

Code compliance in public, rental, supported, and subsidized housing falls under the jurisdiction of property inspectors or code enforcement officials who are mandated to ensure compliance with building and property codes. This is achieved through regular inspections of living units, documentation of specific code violations, and a written action plan that ensures compliance with regulations. Under some circumstances, housing providers are required to provide "reasonable accommodation" for someone whose hoarding is considered to be due to disability. The US Fair Housing Act protects people from discrimination on the basis of disability, including mental disability. This act requires housing providers to make reasonable accommodations for people with disabilities and their families. Some examples of reasonable accommodations for people who hoard include providing access to dumpsters or allowing additional time to deal with the volume of clutter in order to bring the housing unit into compliance with the lease. A disability accommodation is not a "free pass," and housing providers can still impose a fine or other sanctions if the person does not comply with the action plan to meet code requirements.

Public or environmental health

Health officials often become involved in hoarding situations when they receive referrals from other human services professionals such as fire departments or housing agencies, or when they receive complaints from the public. Public health officers can take many roles when working with people who hoard, depending on the nature of the violations and the plans to achieve compliance. Environmental or public health officials are responsible for protecting the health of members of the immediate community as well as the health of people who hoard. They commonly assess the degree of risk to health, such as the presence of mold, insect or rodent infestations, and standing water that promotes disease or attracts vermin. Public health officers assess the home and surrounding property with an eye toward whether a hoarding problem is causing specific health-code violations. They are mandated to assess unsafe situations and monitor progress toward compliance with health codes.

Protective services

Certain groups of citizens are considered special classes who are protected under the law from abuse or neglect that may result from hoarding situations. Children, people with disabilities, and older adults are protected in most jurisdictions. Protective services professionals include social workers and other staff members of child welfare agencies and agencies that serve older adults and/or people with disabilities. These staff members can be contacted directly by concerned citizens or staff from other human services organizations to investigate a situation. Both child and adult protective services workers are empowered to act if they observe imminent threats or risks to the protected group. Depending on the nature and severity of the situation, interventions to correct the risks may be carried out quickly or more slowly and can include temporary removal of the protected individuals (children, older adults, people with disabilities) from the home until the risk has been reduced or eliminated.

Coordinated community services

Professionals from housing, public/environmental health, and protective services have regulatory mandates when addressing problematic hoarding. Their involvement with hoarding cases stems from an apparent need for compliance with legal codes and mandates. Their ability to succeed in eliminating hoarding-related risks is enhanced when referrals come from those who encounter hoarding in the course of their daily work activities (for example, first responders in police and fire departments and emergency medical personnel) and when they work in collaboration with other human services professionals mentioned above who can provide supportive assistance. Accordingly, professionals from the fields of medicine, mental health, occupational therapy, and nursing, along with case managers, in-home support specialists, and professional organizers, can be helpful partners to enforcement agencies in addressing the complexities of severe hoarding situations.

To facilitate speedy interventions, maximize available resources, and achieve productive outcomes, collaborative relationships need to be built among these professionals who bring special expertise to their work on hoarding problems. Addressing severe hoarding is a big task that no single person or professional can do alone. Accordingly, during the past 15 years, many communities throughout North America have formed formal and informal networks of diverse professionals who consult with one another to help people resolve their hoarding. Though each community professional group has its own specific priorities for what changes must be made to meet regulations or the supportive assistance it can provide, working collaboratively within a network of providers allows the person who is hoarding to receive a coordinated message about the priorities for change and the available resources to accomplish the goal(s).

The primary goal for most community human services agencies is to ensure that everyone has a safe place to live. In order to achieve this safety-focused outcome, community agencies must address hoarding behavior even in the context of other challenging problems like dementia, substance use, or homelessness. The goals of coordinated community-based interventions for hoarding typically include decreasing the frequency in the community of severe hoarding cases, improving the health and quality of life of people who hoard and their neighbors, and reducing threats to the general public caused by fire and unsanitary conditions. Short-term aims of community-based hoarding interventions are usually focused on education to increase awareness and provide evidence-based information to front-line service providers and to the community at large. This helps offset myths and negative attitudes about hoarding (for example, "Why can't they just clean it up?" and "A bulldozer would solve this problem") that can impede progress. Of course, in the longer term, all of these human services organizations also seek to minimize hoarding-related budget costs for government organizations, community agencies, and housing providers.

It is important for all community staff members to remember that people who hoard have their own goals as they seek to remain in stable housing, avoid legal sanctions, and become free of monitoring for compliance. When people who hoard have some insight and motivation to use the supportive assistance offered by community human service organizations, they will have additional goals to improve their everyday functioning in daily living and to use the space in their homes as others do—to prepare and eat meals, to invite family and friends over to visit, and so forth. Community support staff such as case managers can be especially helpful in achieving these outcomes that go beyond regulatory compliance and are likely to help maintain the gains.

What community-based supports are available to help with hoarding?

Throughout this book we've highlighted a number of intrapersonal, community, and resource constraints that call for a response to hoarding that extends beyond mental health treatment. In this chapter we've highlighted the unfortunate reality that serious cases of hoarding demand a community enforcement response regardless of the individual's level of insight or motivation. Together, these factors point to the need for community supports for individuals who will not voluntarily seek treatment for their hoarding. Below we highlight five common community-based approaches to hoarding intervention.

Task forces

Coordinated community-based hoarding intervention is commonly achieved through hoarding task forces, also known as hoarding coalitions, networks, or alliances. The first of these efforts began well over a decade ago, and this approach to community interventions has become increasingly popular throughout North American and other parts of the developed world. Task forces are a mechanism by which diverse disciplines come together to address hoarding in the community. For more information about the development and workings of such community task forces, see Dr. Bratiotis and her colleagues' book *The Hoarding Handbook: A Guide for Human Service Professionals.*

Commonly, task forces develop as grassroots efforts because front-line community professionals observe and respond to a need for enhanced communication and coordinated service efforts, or because a hoarding case receives unwanted public attention that drives a community's desire to develop a systematic mechanism for responding to such situations. Hoarding task forces serve various functions: community and professional education, case consultation, direct support for people who hoard, and advocacy for policy change. Task forces establish their purpose and activities to meet local needs and to make use of available resources within a given community. People who hoard may be included as members of their community's task force, ensuring that the voice of people with lived experience is represented in communications, decision making, and intervention efforts. Additionally, task forces can serve as a bridge to other community-based services for hoarding or as a direct provider of such services.

Peer-led and community-based support groups

In an increasing number of communities, support groups for people who hoard are offered through hoarding task forces and human services organizations. Distinct from the clinical group treatment discussed in Chapter 7, these groups are often led by peers and may follow the *Buried in Treasures* self-help book described in Chapter 8. Such groups can also be facilitated by university student volunteers and/or professionals from disciplines other than mental health (for example, occupational therapy or nursing). They vary in length from several weeks to several months. Self-help groups that used *Buried in Treasures* have been systematically studied in both open trials and waitlist comparison trials, with findings showing generally good success: the peer-led groups produced benefits approximately equal to clinical group treatment. Accordingly, this type of intervention can be offered in community settings by trained facilitators from a range of backgrounds. Usually, these groups are offered at reduced or no cost to participants in community settings that are accessible by public transit and feel comfortable to local community members.

In addition to the *Buried in Treasures* groups, some communities also offer a range of non-manualized, unstructured support and/or psychoeducation groups. These groups have not been scientifically studied for effectiveness and vary a great deal in their format, organization, and leadership. At the same time, they appear to fill an important gap in resources for many communities. Cost, lack of available trained clinicians, and stigma associated with seeking mental health services are some of the most common barriers to accessing clinical care. Drop-in support groups are especially nonthreatening and do not require an ongoing commitment, so the barriers to joining are low. They can be an important first self-help step before a person decides to join a *Buried in Treasures* group offered in the community. Some communities also use support groups to reinforce maintenance of benefits after a person completes the more formal *Buried in Treasures* groups. We are aware of at least one ongoing support group that has alternated 3 or 4 months of *Buried in Treasures*–guided work with a few months of general support on hoarding problems before re-engaging group members in *Buried in Treasures*–guided efforts for another few months.

Case management models

Case management is a human services intervention for vulnerable populations who are suffering from serious problems such as mental illness, intimate partner violence, and substance use. Often, the challenges associated with these life problems are better managed and reduced when the sufferer maintains a long-term relationship with a human services professional who help them identify goals, resources, and next steps in their lives. Case managers facilitate access and use of multiple services in order to stabilize health, mental health, and housing needs, among other domains of life. Hoarding is a particularly appropriate target problem for such coordinated human services, and case management is increasingly used as a community-based intervention strategy.

A growing number of task forces, community human services agencies, housing providers, and even clinical treatment centers are offering at least some case-management services for hoarding, although they may not use this term to describe their efforts. The most common case-management activities for people who hoard are case finding, support, assessment, brokering of services, goal setting, monitoring, advocacy, and crisis intervention. One exemplary model of case management for hoarding is offered through Metro Housing Boston's Center for Hoarding Intervention. This unique program uses harm-reduction techniques and cognitive–behavioral therapy (CBT) strategies alongside home-based case-management tools to assist people who hoard in developing the necessary skills to reduce clutter and to maintain stable housing. The effectiveness of Metro Housing Boston's program has been measured both in tenancy preservation and in clutter reduction. Their findings indicated that for 175 clients in supported housing who were served by their hoarding program, 98% were able to meet code requirements and remain in their homes. In addition, their clutter reduced significantly and substantially on the pictorial Clutter Image Rating (by 1.7 points on average).

Unfortunately, apart from the information noted above, the effectiveness of case management for hoarding problems is not clear, as reports are mainly anecdotal. However, in 2016 Dr. Catherine Ayers and her colleagues reported findings from their study of 58 community-dwelling older adults, 27 of whom were randomly assigned to receive case management while the others received a form of CBT (described in Chapter 7). A geriatric nurse provided 45- to 60-minute weekly case-management sessions for 26 weeks that were focused on assessing clients' capacities and particular needs regarding hoarding and other problems, brokering services, providing emotional support, and advocating for clients when problems arose. The results of this study suggest that case management was not as effective as the specialized CBT methods, but 25% of those who received case management showed a decrease in hoarding symptoms. Case management also helped a number of hoarding clients achieve target goals such as improved health outcomes and reduced safety concerns. Case management also served as a conduit for participants to seek additional help for their hoarding through other means.

In-home decluttering

Another community-based strategy sometimes used to help people with hoarding problems is in-home decluttering coaching support. This step-by-step strategy to reduce clutter provides support for the person's efforts to reduce the overall volume of possessions by systematically examining categories of objects, making intentional decisions about whether to keep or discard them, and removing unwanted items and moving kept items to their final destination within the home. This work is often slow and requires patience on the part of the decluttering coach. Appropriate candidates for such coaching roles include (but are not limited to) case managers, peers, volunteers, housing/tenancy support specialists, psychology students, friends, and neighbors. In some instances, family members may also serve as coaches when their relationship to the person with hoarding is positive and generally without conflict. In-home decluttering is usually used to support other intervention methods and has not been studied as a standalone strategy, so unfortunately little can be said about its effectiveness beyond anecdotal reports.

Cleanouts

No doubt the hoarding intervention that comes to mind most commonly for the general public is a home cleanout. Certainly, the several television shows depicting this strategy for clearing clutter in severely hoarded homes have helped cement the image of a cleanout company and junk-removal truck as the "go to" solution for hoarding. However, the success of cleanouts has not been seriously studied as a community-based intervention for hoarding. Only one study conducted nearly two decades ago examined the outcomes for older adults with hoarding problems. Among 7 people whose homes were completely cleared by a professional company, none showed a resolution of the hoarding problem, and for 29 people whose homes were partially cleared, only 17% were able to maintain clutter-free homes by themselves or with the help of a homemaker; the clutter actually worsened for 21%. These findings and general practice experience indicates that involuntary cleaning of the home is not a solution to hoarding problems and should only be used in cases of immediate serious danger to occupants and neighbors. Certainly, cleanouts are ill advised as a sole strategy owing to the loss of control, severe anxiety, loss of valued items, and lack of involvement by the person with the hoarding problem. Some argue that a wholesale cleanout unaccompanied by other skills training and supporting treatment methods constitutes a traumatic life event. At a minimum, a cleanout is likely to engender significant mistrust and anger when future interventions are suggested.

In some circumstances, as described earlier in this chapter, the conditions of the home are so dire that urgent action must be taken to reduce the immediate risk to occupants and neighbors. In some cases, the community organizations and legal entities seeking to resolve a problematic hoarding situation have not considered viable alternatives to a total cleanout of the home, especially when a cleanout can achieve immediate compliance with regulatory mandates. However, educated citizens and family members can and should advocate effectively for a slower systematic reduction of clutter with ongoing monitoring of progress. Until there is greater clarity about the outcomes and effectiveness of cleanouts, this strategy should be considered an intervention of last resort.

Focus on: community responses to hoarding

In some situations, hoarding as a private mental health problem can become a health and safety risk to the community, necessitating a public response from governmental and nongovernmental enforcement and human services organizations. Human services sectors such as housing, public health, and protective services may become involved when risks are imminent and when the welfare of specially protected populations hangs in the balance. The person who hoards can be supported in efforts to regain compliance with regulatory mandates by trained professionals from the fields of nursing, occupational therapy, social work, housing, professional organizing, and others.

A growing number of communities have formed coordinated hoarding response networks, most commonly organized as hoarding task forces. Diverse stakeholders participate in these efforts to develop and deliver accurate community education about hoarding and to coordinate responses to hoarding cases, thereby ensuring that people who hoard receive the most evidence-based, supported, and resourced interventions. Other promising community-based supports for hoarding include case management, peer-led groups, and in-home decluttering assistance. Although these approaches are still understudied, they are increasingly popular in communities across the globe and appear to be important options on the menu of intervention services for hoarding.

10

WHAT ARE THE NEXT STEPS TO UNDERSTAND AND TREAT HOARDING?

What don't we understand about hoarding disorder?

As evident from our previous chapters, there are many aspects of hoarding problems and hoarding disorder (HD) that are not well understood at this time. This chapter discusses several of the main areas of uncertainty about this complex and challenging problem.

Diagnostic criteria for HD

The most recent version of the *Diagnostic and Statistical Manual for Mental Disorders* (DSM-5) from the American Psychiatric Association (see Chapter 1) and the newest version of the International Classification of Disorders (ICD-11) from the World Health Organization differ somewhat in how they define the role of acquisition in HD. Both groups designate HD as an obsessive-compulsive spectrum disorder. However, DSM-5 designates acquiring behavior as a specifier "with acquisition," whereas ICD-11 includes acquiring as a central element in the development of clutter. The draft version of the ICD-11 given in Table 10.1 seems somewhat clearer and therefore preferable to the DSM-5 criteria in describing acquiring as a central element of the accumulation of possessions in HD. Given the very high frequency of acquiring symptoms according to research findings and the importance of treating excessive acquisition

Table 10.1. ICD-11 Criteria for HD

Symptoms and Their Effects	Description of Symptoms
HD is characterized by accumulation of possessions due to excessive acquisition of or difficulty discarding possessions, regardless of their actual value.	
	Excessive acquisition is characterized by repetitive urges or behaviors related to amassing or buying items.
	Difficulty discarding possessions is characterized by a perceived need to save items and distress associated with discarding them.
Accumulation of possessions results in living spaces becoming cluttered to the point that their use or safety is compromised.	
The symptoms result in significant distress or significant impairment in personal, family, social, educational, occupational, or other important areas of functioning.	

in cognitive-behavioral therapy (CBT) models, adopting the ICD-11 diagnostic criteria makes sense for the United States and Canada.

Acquiring behavior

It is also of special interest to better understand acquiring behavior, especially how marketing and consumer behavior contribute to excessive acquisition and the role of acquiring in the development of saving and clutter. In clinical treatment of HD, we have found that treating excessive acquisition early in the process is especially helpful in generating a quick success that motivates clients and stems the tide of incoming items while clients learn skills to help them organize and let go of possessions. A better understanding of acquiring behavior would be helpful to advance progress toward successful outcomes.

Digital hoarding

Digital hoarding has been described in the literature, but very little research has focused on this increasing problem in which people feel compelled to save electronic information and files but do so in such a disorganized fashion that it is difficult to retrieve the content of interest. This behavior does not meet criteria for hoarding because it does not involve acquiring and saving physical objects that clutter the home. However, some individuals find their collecting and saving of digital information to be problematic with regard to time spent, distress and confusion about the information, and difficulty organizing and parting with the items. It seems likely that such behavior will increase in the current digital age, so understanding the sources of this problem and developing interventions will be necessary. Research on digital hoarding has only begun to emerge, with initial efforts aimed at assessing these behaviors and understanding whether they are associated with object hoarding. We look forward to more scientific research on this topic.

Insight and motivation

It is clear that people who hoard often lack insight or awareness of the extent of their mental health problem and sometimes discount the severity of their acquiring, difficulty discarding, and clutter, even when it is abundantly evident to others that the problem is quite serious. Unfortunately, the field struggles with how to assess the degree of insight/awareness and how to use that information to inform treatment, as noted in the section below. Standard methods to assess insight in such disorders as obsessive-compulsive disorder (OCD) do not work well for people with HD, and measures of awareness of illness that are useful for people with severe mental illness (for example, schizophrenia, bipolar disorder, substance use disorders) have not been adapted for hoarding. It would also be helpful to understand what factors increase or decrease motivation, as these could help guide sufferers to the most appropriate interventions.

Use of language about hoarding

Most mental health and social services professionals know that some language is stigmatizing and tends to offend people with hoarding problems and their family members. Examples are "hoarder" to describe a person with lived experience of hoarding, as well as "trash," "junk," or "the hoard" to describe clutter in the home. Even "clutter" can offend some people with HD who describe their saved possessions in different terms. Neutral terms ("your things," "your possessions," "your collections") can be used to match the language being used by the person with the hoarding problem. However, even for an individual who self-describes as "a hoarder," it is wise to avoid that term as it characterizes the whole person by one set of behaviors. Accordingly, an important area for improvement in providing information and intervention to people with hoarding problems is to model the use of respectful language that does not dampen their motivation to work on the problem.

Causes of hoarding behavior

Despite the explosion of research on an array of potential factors pertinent to HD as outlined in previous chapters, much remains to be learned about what features render people vulnerable to hoarding behavior. These include genetics, family history, psychological traits like perfectionism, the role of co-morbid problems such as depression and anxiety, and physical factors. Although it is clear that hoarding occurs across cultures, we know little about specific cultural influences on hoarding. Nor are the effects of marketing and advertising on compulsive acquisition well understood. Likewise, there are significant gaps in our knowledge about cognitive and neuropsychological factors and how these link to emotional and behavioral aspects of hoarding.

Symptoms in diverse populations

It is clear that hoarding occurs across many cultures, as studies of prevalence and features have been conducted in the United States and Canada, Australia, Europe, the Middle East, and Asia, and new research is being published from various countries on an ongoing basis. Missing from the list are African societies, where it is not yet clear whether hoarding occurs, especially in rural agrarian communities. Also missing from most studies in the developed world are diverse samples that represent the population at large, especially with regard to race, ethnicity, and gender, given that men tend to be underrepresented in research samples and some findings indicate they may not benefit as much from CBT interventions as women. It is important to understand possible differences in the manifestations and causes of hoarding among different groups to ensure that interventions appropriately target the symptoms in ways that are likely to be effective.

Hoarding in children

Hoarding develops on average during the teenage years but can appear in younger children as well. Unfortunately, few studies have investigated what triggers excessive collecting and saving behaviors that go well beyond typical childhood actions. Perhaps unexpected loss is a vulnerability factor, as some adults recall that they had lost valued possessions during a family move to a new home when they were young. One woman reported that her grandmother threw away all of her dolls because she thought the girl had too many of them. As a grown woman, her hoarding was very severe and included a collection of several hundred dolls. But it is not clear how often such losses in childhood trigger excessive acquiring and saving and what other vulnerability factors are common among those with hoarding problems. Likewise, there is little research on the best treatment strategies for children. Presumably intervention will involve both the children and their parents or guardians, but what methods are most useful for young children and for teenagers who are advancing toward adulthood?

Animal hoarding

As discussed in Chapter 1, the research on understanding and developing effective interventions for animal hoarding is very limited, probably because it is more difficult to study a problem that involves illegal behavior that jeopardizes the animals' welfare. It is important to confirm empirically whether the proposed categories of overwhelmed caregiver, rescuer, and exploiter are accurate and require similar or different intervention methods. Strategies are needed to recruit people who hoard animals as they are often socially isolated and hide the problem. Only with a better understanding of animal hoarding can we develop effective treatment strategies to improve attitudes, emotions, and behaviors related to animals.

Clinic and community partnerships

Unfortunately, the research literature on hoarding is currently bifurcated with regard to the full spectrum of HD in the population. That is, researchers who work in university and medical clinics recruit voluntary clients who are interested in participating in research and in seeking treatment. In contrast, community studies of hoarding focus on involuntary clients with more limited insight and motivation to work on their problem. These individuals are typically identified by a housing or social services organization due to violations of housing and sanitation codes. Studies that include both voluntary and non-voluntary people with HD are needed to understand the full spectrum of the problem. This might be accomplished by developing shared methods for assessing hoarding symptoms and severity, as well as related features, comorbidity, early history, cognitive functioning, and other factors. This will inevitably involve in-home assessment to verify the hoarding symptoms and state of the home. A further important question is what treatment strategies will work best to improve insight and motivation, as well as symptoms, as discussed further in the next section.

What's missing from the CBT model of HD?

Most of the elements of the CBT model of HD were articulated in Drs. Frost and Hartl's seminal paper in 1996 and slightly revised in a 2003 review by Drs. Steketee and Frost. Many aspects of this theory have been confirmed in scientific testing, and it is clear that the treatments that emerged have been moderately successful in reducing hoarding symptoms. However, the treatment outcomes are not yet compelling, as most people who receive CBT benefit but not to the point that they no longer qualify for an HD diagnosis. This suggests that refining and/or expanding the theory is needed to develop more effective intervention strategies.

What might be added based on what we know so far about hoarding behavior? Three possibilities come to mind, though there are undoubtedly others: addictions, attachment, and consumer economic behavior.

Addictions models

The compulsive acquisition aspect of HD appears similar to experiences of people who are addicted to substances: they behave impulsively and have great difficulty resisting strong urges. Would theories of addictions be useful to better understand hoarding behavior? Unfortunately, the mental health field has only a limited track record of success in treating addictions, so it is not yet clear how theories that included these features would improve outcomes. At the same time, if the addictive behaviors have similar underlying causes, they may help scientists refine our understanding of hoarding.

Human attachment models

Another compelling theory for hoarding is that the early attachment relationships of people who hoard may be compromised so that objects become important substitutes for people. We know that people who hoard have life histories in which various traumas have played a role, although most do not develop post-traumatic stress disorder (PTSD) in which trauma is relived in various ways and emotions are often triggered by reminders of the trauma. If PTSD is rare in HD, might hoarding be an effective compensatory strategy that defends people from greater suffering? Or perhaps the traumas (for example, loss of caretaking figures, chaotic early childhood experiences), while not sufficient (not life threatening) to trigger PTSD, are still emotionally damaging and produce feelings of insecurity that result in collecting and saving objects, as in Kellett's site security model of hoarding. This seems an important avenue to pursue to better understand hoarding behaviors and perhaps especially animal hoarding.

Consumer behavior models

Another area of importance involves consumer behavior; these models are well developed in the field of economics but relatively untested in mental health. This might include concepts such as sensitivity to monetary reward, risk taking, and cognitive assumptions about gains and losses from acquiring, keeping, and discarding items. Further collaborative work by psychologists and economists may help clarify possible factors that contribute to hoarding and may be useful in its treatment.

How can we improve interventions for HD?

As our understanding of hoarding behavior and its origins continues to expand, our ability to provide the best and most helpful interventions will likewise increase in meaningful ways. In this section, we consider some of the next steps the field might take in expanding clinical and community-based hoarding interventions.

Prevention and early intervention

Although recent research suggests that the average age of onset for hoarding behavior is around 17 years, it is often difficult to assess clinical hoarding at this stage of life because the clutter has not yet reached a critical mass and is less likely to interfere in daily life activities. If hoarding is causing some amount of difficulty, efforts by family members to control the clutter may make it difficult to assess the extent of the person's saving behavior. Instead, attending to other prominent features of the problem, such as difficulty letting go of objects, strong emotional attachment, assigning special meanings to things, and indecision, are likely to be better indicators of the potential for developing a hoarding problem. Because hoarding is described as a chronic condition that is unlikely to improve spontaneously, making careful observations of early presentation of symptoms and acting on them sooner rather than later may be an important approach to early intervention.

Research with children who hoard is still early in its development, and until larger-scale studies can be conducted, it will be challenging to establish effective prevention and early intervention protocols. Determining a person's genetic, neurobiological, and cognitive vulnerabilities seems important in identifying potential predictors of hoarding in children, although the science behind this is not yet well established. Longitudinal research that follows children into and through middle adulthood is one method by which the scientific community can expand its knowledge base. Until then, helping children clear accumulated clutter while also attending to underlying beliefs about the objects is likely to forestall the need for later interventions.

Medications

At present, the number of medication trials for hoarding is very limited. Historically, the research was focused on the class of serotonergic medications in samples of people diagnosed with OCD who also had hoarding symptoms. The outcomes of these studies are hard to interpret, given the differences between OCD and hoarding, and the benefits for hoarding symptoms have been modest at best. It is possible that stimulant medications may improve some of the neurocognitive problems associated with hoarding, especially executive functioning difficulties such as attention, decision making, and completing complex tasks. As our understanding of the neuropsychological features of hoarding advances, further testing of this class of medications may teach us more. Improved understanding of the impact of medication as an adjunctive treatment to CBT may also aid sufferers.

Enhancing motivation

Previously, we've commented on the importance of building internal motivation to address hoarding difficulties and noted the value of motivational interviewing (MI) as a distinct set of communication strategies aimed at raising awareness of and resolving ambivalence about hoarding behavior. Current research on MI suggests that it is effective for a range of clinical problems, including both mental and physical health conditions. Two small pilot studies have examined motivation enhancement as part of an intervention for family members of people who hoard, and MI strategies are commonly used during CBT for hoarding in clinical treatment studies. However, whether MI actually improves motivation in people who hoard has not been systematically documented.

Borrowing from clinical treatment approaches, community-based interventions for hoarding also commonly employ MI strategies. The complex circumstances of community-based clients with severe hoarding, especially reluctant or involuntary clients, suggest that the principles and strategies of MI will be especially helpful, although modifications may be needed and some strategies may be more useful than others. Opportunities to test MI methods in the context of community-based hoarding intervention are needed.

Access to services

The best-established clinical treatment for hoarding, specialized outpatient CBT (described in Chapter 7), has advanced our ability to help treatment-seeking individuals, who tend to be more motivated, insightful, and resourced than clients served by community agencies. But there are many people who lack access to CBT for hoarding. The barriers are many. Individual treatment is lengthy (26 sessions) and requires an approximately weekly commitment to attend sessions and complete homework between sessions; this can be cost prohibitive for those whose insurance plans do not cover treatment. In addition, the number of well-trained therapists who understand hoarding and are skilled in delivering CBT is very limited, and they are often concentrated in city centers, leaving outlying areas without trained clinicians. We also suspect that many therapists are reluctant to treat hoarding, finding the problem itself and the accompanying mental and physical comorbidities overwhelming. Reluctant to commit their clinical time to treating HD, they do not seek training in the necessary skills. Some clinicians may also experience practical problems getting out-of-office practice sessions approved for reimbursement by insurance companies. Increasing the number of skilled clinicians is an important next step for professional organizations in this field, along with advocacy for reimbursement by third-party payers.

Alternative delivery strategies for CBT

Beyond the existing individual and group CBT hoarding treatment and the *Buried in Treasures* groups for hoarding, technology-based treatments are beginning to gain ground. Already, online hoarding groups that communicate through a listserv have been providing peer support to people who hoard. Webcam-delivered treatment during which a therapist delivers CBT without leaving the office to a client at home has shown real promise in several cases. This delivery method eliminates some of the treatment access barriers, especially for people in remote areas. It relies on the ability to use appropriate technology, a potential barrier that is relatively easily resolved. Clearly more study of this method is warranted.

In addition, blended in-person and internet-based group CBT for hoarding is in the early phase of development. Two pilot studies have tested the benefits of adding online clinician support to in-person group treatment sessions; both showed promising outcomes for clutter reduction and important process factors like client motivation, group cohesion, and mutual support. Perhaps even more exciting is a recent pilot study of a fully online 20-week group treatment that used webcam and cloud-based video conferencing technology. With technical support from a group facilitator, the participants showed improvement in their hoarding symptoms. The use of technology to deliver mental health services for hoarding is especially exciting given that hoarding behavior takes place mainly in the home or outside acquiring situations. We look forward to more scientific study of these methods.

Alternative methods of treatment

Although CBT for hoarding is the most well-developed and effective treatment to date, there is room for improvement in reducing hoarding symptoms. Better understanding of causal features of the problem will inevitably expand our interest in additional or alternative treatments. Researchers, clinicians, and the general public persist in wondering about the fit for hoarding of theories of addiction, an area worthy of further exploration. Indeed, the MI methods included in CBT are derived directly from motivational work on substance abuse problems. Might hoarding be treated as an addiction to stuff (rather than substances), and furthermore, could acquisition problems benefit from treatments shown effective for the impulse-control problems?

Another possible treatment approach for hoarding yet to be explored is a focus on attachment relationships, perhaps through emotionally focused therapies aimed at helping people develop stronger personal relationships, greater confidence in their decisions, and higher levels of self-esteem. Related to attachment-focused therapies, it is possible that hoarding clients might benefit from processing traumatic loss experiences that predated their hoarding behavior. A final area to mention here is behavioral reinforcement and punishment. Dr. David Tolin's interesting work in this area, which is connected to consumer behavior and the valuing of objects, may guide therapeutic efforts aimed at basic behavioral concepts of reward and punishment.

Stepped-care methods for delivering hoarding intervention

During the early years of research on hoarding, the focus was almost exclusively on establishing that hoarding was a public health problem of significance separate from OCD and that it warranted clinical treatment that provided symptom relief and improved quality of life for people who hoard. We now understand the spectrum of hoarding severity, its accompanying mental and physical health conditions, and the prominent features of limited insight and motivation. Enhanced understanding of this continuum has also directed our attention to those who may not come to clinical or research attention—that is, community-dwelling reluctant and involuntary clients. These individuals often have challenging health and safety risks associated with their hoarding and need intervention options beyond standard mental health treatment, including strategies like harm reduction and case management.

Communities are continuing to expand their coordinated service delivery for people who hoard by actively engaging many different professional groups across service contexts. In order to more comprehensively address both clinic and community-based hoarding situations, a stepped-care model is worthy of careful exploration. Recognizing the impact of degrees of insight and motivation on readiness for change, combined with variable access to evidence-based intervention resources, suggests that people might seek care in a wide variety of ways. For some, readiness/motivation to change begins at a peer-support group, whereas for others a harm-reduction approach through family and friends' support is what's needed. Some people who hoard will be open to a peer-led *Buried in Treasures* group, whereas others are already motivated to seek individual CBT. Entering a system of care at one level may necessitate an eventual "stepping" to a higher level of support for those who need it, although others are able to make and maintain sufficient gains through a single intervention method. The degree of risk, especially severe risk, may demand a higher level of care at the outset in order to eliminate the risk of harm, followed by a step down to lower level of care that includes monitoring and supportive assistance. Conceptualizing, resourcing, and implementing a comprehensive stepped-care model is a significant undertaking for any community. Advocacy and policy development are necessary companions for accomplishing this level of change.

Focus on: next steps in understanding and treating HD

Although a great deal of research has been conducted in the past two decades on hoarding and a new diagnosis of HD has been defined, there remains much to learn about this problem and how best to intervene to resolve the distressing and impairing symptoms. In the general realm of understanding the features of hoarding, more study is needed on clarifying and simplifying the diagnostic criteria, acquiring behavior, digital hoarding, insight and motivation for help, causes, differences across cultures and ethnic groups, children, and animal hoarding. Research on the full spectrum of voluntary and involuntary hoarding can be accomplished through clinic and community partnerships. The existing CBT model of hoarding is compelling, but treatments derived from this model fall short of providing full resolution of HD. Missing from this model may be theories about addictions, attachment to people and objects, and an economic understanding of consumer behavior.

With regard to interventions, more work is needed to develop prevention strategies for those likely to develop the problem, as well as early intervention before middle age, when behaviors are already established and the problem is severe. Additional research on medications may be useful, perhaps derived from a better understanding of the underlying neurocognitive and genetic aspects of hoarding. An ongoing challenge is how to improve insight and motivation so people with hoarding problems can get the help they need and commit to working hard on solutions that improve their lives. This requires access to clinicians and service providers who are trained in the most effective methods for hoarding, which may include various alternative delivery methods for CBT such as web-based individual and group methods. Whether additive or alternative methods will enhance the currently modest benefits of CBT is not yet known. In addition, treatment in mental health clinics is only one method of providing help. It seems likely that multiple professional players from social services, community services, and mental health professions are needed to provide adequate care to the full spectrum of voluntary and involuntary clients who suffer from HD. How best to develop such partnerships requires more work, especially to determine which people will benefit most from which interventions. Stepped-care methods that begin with limited intervention followed by more intensive treatment can be developed.

BIBLIOGRAPHY AND RESOURCES

Books

Bratiotis, C., Schmalisch, C., & Steketee, G. (2011). *The hoarding handbook: A guide for human service professionals.* New York, NY: Oxford University Press.

Frost, R. O., & Steketee, G. (2010). *Stuff: Hoarding and the meaning of things.* New York, NY: Houghton-Mifflin-Harcourt.

Frost, R. O., & Steketee, G. (Eds.) (2014). *Oxford handbook for hoarding and acquiring.* New York, NY: Oxford University Press.

Miller, W. R., & Rollnick, S. (2012). *Motivational interviewing: Helping people change* (3rd ed.). New York, NY: Guilford Press.

Muroff, J., Underwood, P., & Steketee, G. (2014). *Group treatment for hoarding disorder: Therapist guide.* New York, NY: Guilford Press.

Snowdon, J., Halliday, G., & Banerjee, S. (2012). *Severe domestic squalor.* New York, NY: Cambridge University Press.

Steketee, G., & Frost, R. O. (2014). *Treatment for hoarding disorder: Therapist guide* (2nd ed.). New York, NY: Oxford University Press.

Steketee, G., & Frost, R. O. (2014). *Treatment for hoarding disorder: Workbook* (2nd ed.). New York, NY: Oxford University Press.

Tolin, D. T., Frost, R. O., & Steketee, G. (2014). *Buried in treasures: Help for compulsive acquiring, saving, and hoarding.* New York, NY: Oxford.

Tolin, D. F., Worden, B. L., Wooten, B. M., & Gilliam, C. M. (2017). *CBT for hoarding disorder: A group therapy program therapist guide.* Hoboken, NJ: Wiley.

Tompkins, M. A., & Hartl, T. L. (2009). *Digging out: Helping your loved one manage clutter, hoarding, and compulsive acquiring.* Oakland, CA: New Harbinger.

Monographs/Reports

Metro Boston Housing Partnership. (2015). *Rethinking hoarding intervention.* http://www.metrohousingboston.org/wp-content/uploads/2017/10/Hoarding-Report-2015_FINAL.pdf

Patronek, G. J., Loar, L., & Nathanson, N. N. (Eds.) (2006). *Animal hoarding: Structuring interdisciplinary responses to help people, animals and communities at risk.* Hoarding of Animals Research Consortium. https://vet.tufts.edu/wp-content/uploads/AngellReport.pdf

Additional self-help books

Bubrick, J., Neziroglu, F., & Yaryura-Tobias, J. (2004). *Overcoming compulsive hoarding: Why you save and how you can stop.* New York, NY: New Harbinger.

Kolberg, J., & Nadeau, K. G. (2016). *ADD-friendly ways to organize your life.* New York, NY: Routledge.

Zasio, R. (2012). *The hoarder in you: How to live a happier, healthier, uncluttered life.* New York, NY: Rodale.

Journals

American Journal of Psychiatry
Behaviour Research and Therapy
British Journal of Psychiatry
Clinical Psychology Review
Depression and Anxiety
Families in Society
Health and Social Work
Journal of Anxiety Disorders
Journal of Clinical Psychiatry
Journal of Clinical Psychology
Journal of Obsessive Compulsive and Related Disorders
Psychiatric Times
Psychiatry Research

Websites

Hoarding of Animals Research Consortium: https://vet.tufts.edu/hoarding/

International OCD Foundation hoarding website: https://hoarding.
  iocdf.org/
Mass Housing hoarding information: https://www.masshousingrental.
  com/portal/server.pt/community/community_services/330/
  hoarding_resources

Web Apps
Clutter Image Rating (Apple; free)
Life-Pod (Apple and Android; free)
Sortly: Best Declutter App for Keeping a Household Inventory (visual
  inventory of possessions; Apple; free)

INDEX